The Power of
ONE ANOTHER

The Power of ONE ANOTHER

Bob Russell

with Rusty Russell

Standard
PUBLISHING
CINCINNATI, OHIO

All Scripture quotations, unless otherwise indicated, are taken from
the HOLY BIBLE, NEW INTERNATIONAL VERSION®. NIV®.
Copyright © 1973, 1978, 1984 by International Bible Society.
Used by permission of Zondervan.
All rights reserved.

ISBN 0-7847-7199-5

Edited by Lynn Perrigo
Cover design by Liz Howe Design

Standard Publishing, Cincinnati, Ohio
A division of Standex International Corporation
© 2004 by Standard Publishing
All rights reserved
Printed in the United States of America

Contents

INTRODUCTION

What Is Your Church Known For?

A friend of mine preached for years in a troubled church. He once said, "Bob, I noticed in your church paper one of your church's slogans is Speaking the Truth in Love. We don't have a church slogan, but if we did it would be, "If you want to fight, come to First Christian!"

What is your church noted for? If I were to visit your community and ask people about your church, what would they say? "That's the church with a nice building"? "That's the church with good programming"? "That's a Bible-believing church"? "That's the church that bickers a lot"?

I'm invited by a lot of churches to come and talk to them about church growth. One of the first things I tell them is that the church will not stay healthy and grow without love. The place to begin to improve your congregation is not with programs or organization or even doctrine but with the attitude of the people toward one another. Paul took an entire chapter of 1 Corinthians—chapter 13—to convince the Christians in Corinth that they could have all the gifts in the world—the best preachers, the best worship leaders, even supernatural gifts like healing and speaking in tongues—but if they didn't have love, they were just making a bunch of noise, and God wasn't going to bless them. He did the same thing in the book of Romans, taking most of chapter 12 to teach the Roman Christians how to love one another.

I doubt that God has ever blessed a contentious church. Jesus said, "A new command I give you: Love one another. As I have loved you, so you must love one another. By this all men will know that you are my disciples, if you love one another" (John 13:34, 35). Is your church known as a loving church?

Several times in the New Testament the phrase "one another" or "one to another" or "each other" is repeated. The New Testament writers reminded us over and over to love one another, accept one another, serve one another, comfort one another, forgive one another, honor one another, bear one another's burdens, encourage one another, pray for one another, and be kind to one another. In a sense, if you get the first one right—love one another—the rest should fall into place. The rest of those phrases help us define what love looks like in the church.

This book is about those "one another" directives in the New Testament. Jesus said that the world would believe in Him if we were united (John 17:21). Evangelism begins with loving one another. Remember that old camp song that ended, "and they'll know we are Christians by our love"? It's true. The church can turn the world upside down if Christians will love one another.

We're thankful for the opportunity to publish another Bible study book with Standard Publishing. Each of the ten chapters in this book is a look at one of the "one another" passages in the New Testament. Each chapter also covers an event in the life of Christ, showing how He exemplified that particular "one another" passage and encouraging us to imitate His actions. Rusty and I are honored that you would purchase our book. We hope it serves as a good tool for your small group Bible study, Sunday school class, preaching series, or personal devotional time. May we all get a glimpse of what the church ought to be, and may God bless our efforts to love one another!

1

Love One Another

W. Carl Ketcherside was a popular Christian speaker some people referred to as the Apostle of Love. He dedicated himself to breaking down barriers between church groups by proclaiming the love of Christ. There was a woman in his congregation who was totally obnoxious. She was critical, sarcastic, and negative. He once prayed, "Lord, why do You make people like that?" The Lord responded, "Ketcherside, you're so big about loving everybody, I just wanted to see what you could do with her!"

When you come to Christ, you have a new nature and a greater capacity to love others through the power of the Holy Spirit. But that doesn't mean it's going to come easily. You will still find some people difficult to love. Maybe a coworker or a competitor gets on your nerves. Maybe a neighbor won't stay off your grass. Maybe it's a member of your own family—a sarcastic teenager or a mother-in-law who won't hold her tongue. Or maybe it's a person in your congregation—an elder who is critical, a leader who has offended you, or a member whose lifestyle isn't consistent with what he says he believes.

The Characteristics of Christian Love

In Romans 12:10, the apostle Paul wrote, "Be devoted to one another in brotherly love." In the surrounding verses, Paul gave us instructions on how to love each other.

Love Is Authentic

"Love must be sincere," Paul wrote (Romans 12:9). My brother John Russell preaches at the Lakeside Christian Church in Northern Kentucky. He tells about a time when he was out of town visiting another congregation. The effervescent worship leader introduced the greeting time by saying, "I want everyone to turn around and tell the person behind you, 'I love you.'" Sitting in front of John was a beautiful young woman. She turned around, looked deep into John's eyes, and said, "I love you." John's wife Susan grabbed his arm and said back to the young woman, "*We* love you, too"!

Anyone can say, "I love you." You can even say that to a perfect stranger. But Christian love is to be authentic. The Greek word for *sincere* in Romans 12:9 is *anupokritos*. Literally, it means "not hypocritical." A "hupocritos" was a Greek actor, a thespian, who would come onto the stage wearing the mask of comedy and everyone would laugh. Then he would put on the mask of tragedy and everyone would weep. He was a mask wearer. Paul said love is to be sincere—*anupokritos*—no masks.

When a member of our church, Stan Mason, was dying of cancer at his home, dozens of people from church rallied to assist his family. Three of his friends—Mike Veal, Dan Garcia, and Russ Summay—sat with Stan many evenings or even through the night the last two weeks of his life. That's more impressive when you know something about those men—they are *Dr.* Mike Veal, *Dr.* Dan Garcia, and *Dr.* Russ Summay. They get paid for visiting sick people, and it would be easy for them to have a callused attitude about someone's last days of life.

But at no cost, they came and spent many hours trying to ease his pain and comfort the family. That's sincere love.

Love Is Discerning

A young woman in our church was talking to some friends when she pointed out that she believed the lifestyle of a certain Hollywood actress was "wrong." Her friends reprimanded her for daring to judge someone else's behavior, even though the actress has openly and defiantly led a sinful lifestyle. How hypocritical of her friends to so harshly judge her for being judgmental! The postmodern world insists that we shouldn't judge any action as right or wrong. "Let everyone do his own thing," they say. In their minds, the only sin is *intolerance*. So they refuse to tolerate the intolerant—how inconsistent!

"Hate what is evil; cling to what is good," Paul wrote (Romans 12:9). If you love someone, you despise anything that is a threat to his or her well-being. If you love your child, you hate leukemia. If you love your grandmother, you hate Alzheimer's. If you love your mate, you hate cancer. When you understand that sin is lethal, you begin to hate sin while you still love the sinner.

I recently attended the funeral of an AIDS victim who committed suicide. How loving is it to tolerate homosexuality when he could have avoided a dreaded disease if he had remained celibate? When you see the ramifications, it's not difficult to hate homosexuality but still love the person who has engaged in homosexual behavior.

Proverbs 6:16-19 says there are seven things God hates: "Haughty eyes, a lying tongue, hands that shed innocent blood, a heart that devises wicked schemes, feet that are quick to rush into evil, a false witness who pours out lies and a man who stirs up dissension among brothers." God hates sin because He loves those who are hurt by it. Christian love, like God's love, hates that which can harm the one you love. So love has checkpoints and cares about a person's character.

Love cares enough to say, "Hey, that's wrong. I hope you'll stop," when someone is engaging in destructive behavior.

In another passage, Paul commanded, "Brothers, if someone is caught in a sin, you who are spiritual should restore him gently" (Galatians 6:1). He didn't say to ignore the sin, or to condemn the sinner. Christian love encourages repentance and restoration. James concluded his book with these words: "Whoever turns a sinner from the error of his way will save him from death and cover over a multitude of sins" (5:20).

Love Is Loyal

Paul continued, "Be devoted to one another in brotherly love" (Romans 12:10). I can criticize my brother John. I know his faults. I tease him a lot. But I will also go to the mat for him because brothers are loyal.

When Simon Peter betrayed Jesus, he went out and wept bitterly. When you are disloyal, you feel terrible about yourself. You divide relationships and hurt the ones you love. Loyalty holds relationships together through difficult times.

I love the old story of the man who, near the end of his life, looked at his wife and said, "Margaret, you have always been beside me."

"Yes, dear, that's right," his wife replied.

"When I was a young man and couldn't get a job, there you were, right beside me."

"That's right," Margaret said.

"When we bought our first house and the roof leaked and we lost all that money, you were there beside me," he continued. "And when the house burned down, you were there beside me. And then when I got older and needed to retire, and I discovered too late that I didn't have a good pension, you were there beside me. And when I had my heart attack, there you were. During all those weeks in recovery and through another heart attack and bypass surgery, you were there all along the way."

"That's right," Margaret said.

"Margaret," the man said, "I've concluded something: You're bad luck!"

Most of us recognize that a person who sticks beside us through good times and bad is not "bad luck," but loyal.

Jonathan and David were best friends. Jonathan's father, King Saul, hated David and expressed to his son his desire to have David killed. Jonathan could have kept his mouth shut and been the next king of Israel, but he risked his life to tell David about his father's evil intentions because love is loyal (1 Samuel 20). The Bible says, "A friend loves at all times, and a brother is born for adversity" (Proverbs 17:17).

Love Is Unselfish

"Honor one another above yourselves," Paul commanded (Romans 12:10).

I heard about two little girls who were both trying to ride a mechanical rocking horse. One of girls quipped, "If one of us would get off, there'd be more room for me."

The Bible says, "Do nothing out of selfish ambition or vain conceit, but in humility consider others better than yourselves. Each of you should look not only to your own interests, but also to the interests of others" (Philippians 2:3, 4). The world's concept of love is often self-centered: You turn me on, you make me feel good when I'm with you, you light up my life, and therefore I love you. When someone no longer does those things for us, the world says it's OK to stop loving. But Christian love should be different. It's self-sacrificing.

Paul attempted to prove his love for the Thessalonians by reminding them of the sacrifices he made for them. He wrote,

> You know we never used flattery, nor did we put on a mask to cover up greed—God is our witness. We were not looking for praise from men, not from you or anyone else. As apostles of Christ we could have been a burden to you, but we were gentle among you, like a mother caring for her little children. We loved you so much that we were

delighted to share with you not only the gospel of God but
our lives as well, because you had become so dear to us
(1 Thessalonians 2:5-8).

This kind of self-sacrificing love is usually evidenced in the
little things we do every day. For example, I take a shower in
the morning and when I'm done, I reach for a towel. There are
only two towels left—one that is thin and frayed, and another
that is fluffy and soft. I know someone else is getting ready to
shower after me. No one will ever know if I took the better
towel. I've got a decision to make: Who comes first?

It's hard for me to think of a better example of simple
unselfishness than the story I've told for years about my wife.
Once she was fixing dinner and pouring each of us a soft drink,
not knowing I was observing her. Before opening a new two-
liter bottle, she emptied the remains of an old two-liter from
the refrigerator into the first glass. The soft drink was totally
flat—not a bubble of fizz. I thought to myself, *I hope I don't get
that glass.* I watched as she placed that glass in front of her own
table setting. Nobody would have ever known, but she sacrificed for the good of others. Most of us would have secretly
placed it in front of someone else's place, or put a little bit in
everybody's glass to be "fair," or thrown it out! But not my
wife. I wonder how many times she's sacrificed for me, and I
didn't even know it.

When nobody's looking, are you self-sacrificing or self-
serving? Love is unselfish. Someone wrote,

> The test of a man's devotion will come some other day;
> They love God most
> Who are at their post
> When the crowds have gone away.

One recent Friday morning, I arrived about a half-hour early
for a breakfast meeting at a church in Seattle, Washington. I
sneaked into the sanctuary to read over my notes for the talk I

was about to give. As I sat down in the back pew, I was sur-prised to hear the strains of the church organ that early in the morning. I deduced that the organist was practicing for the Sunday worship service. I recognized the familiar chorus of the hymn, "Turn Your Eyes Upon Jesus." It sounded beautiful to me, but there was one phrase the organist wasn't satisfied with. She would play the chorus and then stop at that phrase, make a notation, start over again and stop again at that same phrase. She played the same phrase for nearly twenty minutes, trying to get it right. When she played that thirty-second refrain on Sunday morning, I doubt that anyone in the congregation realized the amount of time she spent to make that one small part of the service excellent. Some might label her obsessive-compulsive, but I thought it was a good example of someone who loved the Lord and God's people so much that she was willing to unselfishly give of her time to make the worship service the best it could be.

When I consider how many people in our congregation vol-unteer their time and energy to help the church function, there are more examples of unselfishness than I could count, as I'm sure there are in your church as well. So many people work behind the scenes, sacrificing and doing things with excellence, even though nobody ever pats them on their backs or recog-nizes what they're doing. People prepare rooms, clean win-dows, practice instruments, study for children's lessons, park cars, take communion to shut-ins, counsel the hurting, paint walls, and do dozens of other things—some very significant and others seemingly insignificant—out of the goodness of their hearts because they love the Lord and love others.

An Illustration of Christian Love

A lawyer came to Jesus and asked, "Teacher, what must I do to inherit eternal life?" (Luke 10:25). That's not a bad question. In fact, it's the most important question you can ask. If there is a world beyond the grave (and there is) and it's worth going to (and it is), then how do I get there?

Jesus didn't answer right away. He decided to draw the man out to see if he would be able to answer it on his own. "What does the law say?" Jesus challenged, knowing the man was an expert in the law. This attorney knew the Torah—the first five books of the Scripture—backward and forward. So Jesus, being the perfect teacher, led the man to discover the answer on his own.

The lawyer answered, "'Love the Lord your God with all your heart and with all your soul and with all your strength and with all your mind'; and, 'Love your neighbor as yourself.'" Good answer. Jesus agreed and commended the man for his wise response. The entire law of God can be summarized in those two phrases, but the lawyer wasn't finished.

"Who exactly is my neighbor?" he asked.

Another good question. Who is my neighbor? Am I in the clear if I love the family next door? What about my boss—do I have to love him? Is he my neighbor too? And how about those foreigners who worked on my roof? They live so far away and they speak a different language. . . . Do I have to get to know them too? Do I have to love them?

To answer the question, Jesus told a story that most would agree is the greatest illustration of neighborliness ever told.

A Person in Need

Jesus said, "A man was going down from Jerusalem to Jericho, when he fell into the hands of robbers. They stripped him of his clothes, beat him and went away, leaving him half dead" (Luke 10:30). The road from Jerusalem to Jericho snakes seventeen miles through a wilderness of rocks and ravines. It was notoriously a hangout for hardened criminals who would lie in wait for any person traveling alone. The seventeen-mile stretch had earned the nickname, "The way of blood."

Our world can be a brutal, violent place. There are murders, kidnappings, muggings, rapes, wars, and abuse every day. The

Bible says, "There will be terrible times in the last days. People will be lovers of themselves, lovers of money, boastful, proud, abusive, disobedient to their parents, ungrateful, unholy, without love, unforgiving, slanderous, without self-control, brutal, not lovers of the good, treacherous, rash, conceited, lovers of pleasure rather than lovers of God" (2 Timothy 3:1-4).

Late one night when I was a student at Cincinnati Bible College, my roommate called me and said he had run out of gas at Eighth and State in downtown Cincinnati. It was a rough section of town, but I knew I had to go help my friend. As I waited for him to start his car, three guys came out of a bar nearby. One of them jumped me. I was punched and beaten before I even knew what hit me, and the guy's ring cut me across the face. It was hard to explain to my theology professors the next day why I had gotten beat up in downtown Cincinnati!

The world can be a bad neighborhood at times, and the victims need our love and care. Churches need to continue to reach out through missions to refugees, ministries to abused wives, prison ministries, hospital ministries, and so on. Many people, however, have never suffered physical harm but are emotionally wounded. As bad as it feels to get beat up, those physical scars heal much quicker than emotional wounds do. When a child grows up in an abusive home, or a husband constantly berates his wife, or a boss prides himself in belittling those beneath him, the wounds that are left behind can run very deep. Mother Teresa said, "The greatest poverty of all is the feeling of being unwanted, uncared for, deserted and alone." The church needs to be alert to ways to minister to those with emotional wounds as well through Christian counseling and creative outreaches like support groups, home fellowship meetings, and accountability groups.

The worst kinds of wounds, however, are spiritual wounds. The thieves in the parable of the Good Samaritan represent Satan, the adversary of Christ, who "was a murderer from the beginning . . . the father of lies" (John 8:44), who "comes only to steal and kill and destroy" (John 10:10). You can see physical wounds, and you can sometimes sense emotional wounds, but many are blind to the spiritual mugging that has taken place in their lives. In Luke 16, Jesus told a story about a rich man who died and went to Hades, and in torment begged for relief. While he was on earth, Satan was his master, and Satan robbed him of eternal life without him even knowing it. He thought all was well, but when he died, he discovered he was spiritually bankrupt.

No matter what kind of wounds our neighbor has—physical, emotional, or spiritual—Jesus calls us to reach out in love. But just like the religious leaders in Jesus' parable, we sometimes get too busy and ignore the needs of those around us.

Two Busy Religious Leaders

The wounded man on the Jericho road heard footsteps coming. I imagine that with every ounce of strength he had, he turned his head and opened his eyes to see who was coming. A man in religious garb. *Thank God!* he must have thought. *Surely he will stop and help me!* But when the priest saw the man, he walked by on the other side of the road. *Help!* the man must have whispered. It did no good. The religious leader hurried on.

The priest was probably exhausted from a long day at the temple. He'd spent the day teaching, saying prayers, offering incense and sacrifices to God. Now he was off duty and on his way home to Jericho. He had told his family he'd be home by dusk, and he knew he had to hurry to make it. When he heard the guttural moans coming from the roadside ahead, he looked and saw a clump of naked flesh, a man who had been beaten raw, seepage of blood and dirt beneath him.

The priest paused for a brief moment and then hurried on, thinking of all the reasons he shouldn't stop. *It could be dangerous,* he probably reasoned. *What if the robbers are still nearby? What if it's a trap? Surely, a group of people not traveling alone will soon come who can help, or the roadside assistance crew will arrive. I can't stop now. I've got to get home—I promised my wife! It's my duty to be a good family man, to keep my word! Besides, if he's really that badly beaten, he's going to die anyway, and I'm not allowed to touch a dead body or I'll be unclean for seven days.*

Then along came a Levite. By this time, the beaten man was probably skeptical. *Oh no, not another religious leader,* he must have thought. The Levite was subordinate to the priest—an associate minister. He, too, was very busy and exhausted from a long day. Maybe he knew the priest was ahead of him and saw the priest pass the man by. He probably thought, *I bet there's a good reason he didn't stop. If he didn't stop, I don't think I should have to. I'd better keep going.*

I can understand the reasoning of the priest and Levite. When I was in Kenya several years ago, we traveled from Nairobi to Narok on a winding, narrow road. The missionary who was driving said, "This is dangerous territory. Several months ago, a missionary couple stopped to help a woman who appeared to be stranded by the side of the road, but bandits jumped out of the woods, raped and killed the missionary's wife, and nearly beat the husband to death. We don't want to be out here at night." I wasn't fond of being out there in the middle of the afternoon! "So if we see someone lying in the road," the missionary continued, "we're not stopping."

It took us longer to reach our destination than we thought it would, so the last hour of the trip we were traveling in the dark. We came across a small truck that was stopped in the middle of the road. Six or seven people were standing around waving for us to stop and help. None of us in the vehicle protested when the missionary cruised right on by. The priest and Levite were wrong to pass by a person in need, but I can sympathize with their actions.

An Unlikely Helper

The wounded man was finally saved by the most unlikely of people—a Samaritan. Jesus said, "But a Samaritan, as he traveled, came where the man was; and when he saw him, he took pity on him" (Luke 10:33).

Notice three positive facts about the Samaritan that should teach us something about what Jesus means when He commands us to love one another.

The Samaritan cared about a man he had never met. He didn't check to see if the beaten man was someone he might know. The plight of a fellow human being in trouble was enough to stir his conscience.

My son Phil is a police officer in our community. In his first weeks on the job, he and his partner happened upon an apartment fire and were able to rescue a man just as the building filled with smoke. Phil was nominated to receive a lifesaving medal for his heroic deed. Most policemen work their entire lives dreaming of being able to save someone's life and get that award; and my son got it in his first weeks on the job! His fellow officers didn't know whether to congratulate him or punch him!

Whenever tragedy strikes—whether it is a terrorist attack, a violent hurricane, a devastating fire, or other calamity—there are always stories of heroes who came to the rescue. A fireman, a policeman, or a total stranger lays his life on the line to save the life of another.

But perhaps even more heroic are those who risk their lives to save the souls of others—often total strangers. Some friends of ours in Romania relate that during the government oppression they had endured for years, Bibles were very scarce. Christians would tear pages out of the Bible, pass them around, and hide them so that they could have them to read. Recently, their church in Romania began a building program and, while digging some footers, discovered a metal container that had been buried in 1937. It had dozens of little blue Bibles in it and a note that said, "We know that in the near future we will no longer be allowed to worship God freely. It is our prayer that you will find these Bibles at a time when our people most need the Word of God." It's been said that a man stands tall who plants a tree in whose shade he never intends to sit. Those Romanians in 1937 went to considerable expense and risk to help save the souls of a generation of total strangers.

The Samaritan assisted a man who was his natural enemy.
The Samaritan bent down and discovered the injured man was
a Jew. If Jesus were telling the story to a group of Jewish people
today, He might say, "Then along came an Arab." If He was
telling the story in a white southern church in the 1950s, He'd
say, "Then along came a black man." He might say to American
Christians today, "Then along came a Muslim."

The Jews and Samaritans hated each other. They refused to
deal with each other. It was said that a Jew would rather eat
with swine than a Samaritan. Remember when Jesus stopped
and talked with the woman at the well in Samaria? His disciples were dumbfounded that He would talk to a Samaritan.
But in Jesus' parable, it was the Samaritan who refused to turn
away from an injured Jew though that man's people had
despised and rejected him.

A few years ago when I was visiting a maximum-security
prison in Eddyville, Kentucky, I met a most impressive man.
He was serving as a volunteer chaplain to the men on death
row. His ministry started over a decade earlier when his
daughter was murdered. To release his bitterness, he went to
visit with and pray for her murderer. That experience motivated him to begin an ongoing ministry of compassion to the prisoners on death row—those he had previously considered the
scum of the earth and his natural enemies.

God asks us to minister to people who are opposed to us,
who resist and criticize us. You know why He wants us to do
that? Because He loves us even though we're so selfish and
ungrateful. The Bible says, "But God demonstrates his own
love for us in this: While we were still sinners, Christ died for
us" (Romans 5:8). "As I have loved you," Jesus said, "so you
must love one another" (John 13:34).

**The Samaritan sacrificed himself for a man who could not
repay him.** The man was not only injured, he was broke. He
had just been robbed. The Samaritan gave of his own resources
with no hope of repayment. Jesus concluded the story by
describing how the Samaritan helped the beaten man: "He

went to him and bandaged his wounds, pouring on oil and wine. Then he put the man on his own donkey, took him to an inn and took care of him. The next day he took out two silver coins and gave them to the innkeeper. 'Look after him,' he said, 'and when I return, I will reimburse you for any extra expense you may have'" (Luke 10:34, 35).

This act of love cost the Samaritan in several expensive ways.

- It cost him time. I'm sure he had a schedule to keep, but he stopped anyway. Opportunities to show love often express themselves at first as interruptions to our plans.
- It also cost him resources. He raced to the man's side and poured wine on his wounds to disinfect them, and then he poured oil on them to soothe them. Those substances weren't cheap, and the oil and wine may have been very precious to him.
- It cost him energy. He shouldered the man and lifted him onto his donkey, and he walked beside the donkey the rest of the journey.
- It cost him sleep. He spent the night watching over him during those first critical twenty-four hours.
- It cost him money. In the morning, he gave the innkeeper two silver coins—two denarii—to pay for the hotel room. That's two days' wages! Hotels were expensive back then too!
- It also cost him indebtedness. He said, "Take care of this man until he is well—whatever it takes. I'll be back through here in a couple of days and I'll pay the bill. Charge it to my account." He obligated himself for any additional expenses the innkeeper might incur. He was willing to go in debt rather than take a chance that the man's needs wouldn't be met. That was a lot of trust! He risked being taken advantage of by the innkeeper or the beaten man.

I love the old story of the oil executive who was touring the Far East when he was invited to visit a leper colony. There he saw a number of pitiful, terminally ill patients. The westerner couldn't get over the sight of a missionary who was squatting down in front of a loathsome leper, binding up the open, repulsive wounds. The executive turned away in disgust, saying, "I wouldn't do that for a million dollars." The missionary overheard him and said quietly, "Neither would I. But I do it for Jesus."

Jesus is our Good Samaritan. We were beaten by sin, robbed of our relationship with God, and left to die an eternal death. But Jesus bent down to this world, spent His last resource—His very life—to save us and nurture us back to spiritual health and give us eternal life. And He says to us, "Go and do likewise" (Luke 10:37).

The great old Baptist preacher Roy Angell suggested that this parable presents the three dominant philosophies of life: The thieves say, "What's yours is mine and I'll take it." The religious leaders say, "What's mine is mine and I'll keep it." The Samaritan says, "What's mine is yours and I'll share it."[1] Which will it be for you? Will you give up yourself and love others in the name of Jesus?

2

Accept One Another

The most revered word in the English language today may be the word *tolerance*. We have diversity training, multicultural events, fairness ordinances, and quotas to encourage us to be tolerant of people who are different. But much of the world's effort toward tolerance is forced and hypocritical, and often serves to alienate people instead of enriching relationships. People call for tolerance while practicing intolerance. For example, when Ellen DeGeneres's character became the first lead character to admit being gay on national television, the show ended with her partner saying, "Let's go out and terrorize some Baptists!" The audience roared with approving laughter. What would happen if a preacher closed his sermon by saying, "Let's go out and terrorize some homosexuals"? His community would be rightly outraged because such an attitude is politically and spiritually incorrect. Much of what masks as tolerance is a disguised attempt to advance a political or moral agenda.

The definition of the word *tolerance* has changed. When our grandparents spoke of tolerance as a virtue, they meant we should respect people and treat them kindly even when we think they're wrong. Postmodern tolerance means never thinking anyone's beliefs or actions are wrong in the first place. So everyone is tolerated except those of us who claim certain actions or beliefs are "wrong."

There is a positive side to this move toward tolerance in our culture. We have become more intolerant of certain sins like racial discrimination that have at times marred the history of our great nation. The Bible commands us to "accept one another" (Romans 15:7) and not show favoritism (James 2:1). Hundreds of years before it became politically correct, Jesus and His followers were urging us to practice tolerance. Jesus himself exemplified this virtue in John 4. He crossed paths with a very unlikely disciple, but to the amazement of His followers, He accepted the woman He met at the well anyway. His example should encourage us to practice genuine tolerance and acceptance of those who are different from us.

The Barriers That Separated Her From Jesus

There were several barriers that made this woman's potential for discipleship very unlikely.

Racial Barrier

First, there was a serious racial barrier. "Jews do not associate with Samaritans," John noted parenthetically (4:9). As I mentioned in the last chapter, a venomous hatred existed between Jews and Samaritans. It had begun 750 years earlier when the Assyrians took the Israelites captive. After years of enduring hardship in prison camps, they were released and allowed to return to Jerusalem. When they arrived back home, they discovered that many of their countrymen who had been left behind had intermarried with the surrounding pagans and had assimilated some of their religious practices. Since Jewish law forbade intermarrying, the loyal Jews regarded intermarriage as intolerable and shunned those who had betrayed them, refusing to allow them to participate in the rebuilding of the city of Jerusalem. The shunned half-Jews settled in Samaria. The Samaritans were despised by even the most tolerant of the Jews.

After years of name-calling and mounting hostilities, the Samaritans galled the Jews even further by daring to build their own temple on Mt. Gerazim and claiming it as the dwelling place of God. "Go ahead and worship in Jerusalem," the Samaritans scoffed. "Mt. Gerazim is where God got His dust to make Adam, where Noah's ark landed, and where Abraham offered Isaac. It's where the true worshiper meets God." Their defiance grated at the Jews who proudly believed God dwelled only in the temple at Jerusalem.

By New Testament times, the racial hatred was so intense that Jews traveling from Jerusalem to Galilee refused to take the direct route through Samaria lest they come into contact with the Samaritan people and become contaminated. Instead of heading north, they traveled eastward many miles out of their way until they crossed the Jordan River. Then they headed northward along the river until they had passed by Samaria safely and could cross the Jordan and travel westward into Galilee. The few extra miles were worth the trouble to any Jew so that he could avoid rubbing shoulders with Samaritans.

But John tells us Jesus *had* to go through Samaria (4:4). It was not a geographical necessity—it was a divine imperative. Jesus refused to go out of His way to avoid certain people. He *had* to take the occasion to demonstrate God's universal appeal, God's love for all the races. He *had* to protest their prejudice and pride.

Gender Barrier

In this day of the liberated female, it's difficult for us to relate to the extreme prejudice that existed against women in Jesus' day. Some strict Jews thanked God in daily prayers that they weren't born "a Gentile or a woman." According to Jewish religious rules, a rabbi was not to have a public conversation with a woman, not even his wife or sister. Rabbi Aboth had written,

"He who talks much with a woman brings evil upon himself and neglects the study of the law, and at the last will inherit Gehenna."[2] In the minds of many Jewish men, women were second-class citizens with no rights and no dignity. Just a cut above the animals, women existed for the convenience of men.

But when this Samaritan woman came to draw water, Jesus treated her as a person worthy of courtesy and respect. Some uninformed critics of Christianity say the Bible is repressive toward women, but just the opposite is true. Jesus elevated the status of women. He treated them with respect and compassion, which was unheard of in His day.

Spiritual Barrier

There was also a spiritual barrier between Jesus and this woman. She was a sinful woman. Her life had been a series of failures, bad decisions, and rejection. She'd tried marriage several times—five to be exact—but it never worked out. Somebody said she had a wash-and-wear wedding gown! She'd finally given up on marriage, but in her loneliness she continued to make bad choices. She was now cohabiting with her new boyfriend. A respectable Jewish rabbi wouldn't be caught speaking to such a woman in public. It would destroy his reputation.

A man once called me and asked if I would talk about Christianity to an erotic dancer he had met. Her life was at the bottom and she had nowhere to turn. She wasn't spiritually sensitive, but she needed help. She said she didn't feel comfortable coming to a church service, but she'd be willing to talk to the preacher. I agreed to the appointment, but she canceled at the last minute. I was kind of relieved because I wondered what the other staff members would think when they saw her walk out of my office!

A Christian businessman told me that he felt convicted that he should be a better witness for Jesus. He went downtown and saw a homeless man sitting on a park bench. He decided to approach him, intending to talk to him about the gospel. Just as he got a few feet away, he looked up to see a professor he knew from the University of Louisville walking toward him. He walked past the man on the bench and spoke to the professor. He couldn't bring himself to be associated with the derelict in the presence of someone he respected.

Jesus didn't care about people's criticisms. He was more concerned about the soul of this sinful woman, and He longed to give her the water of life.

Overcoming the Barriers

Jesus Reached Out in Love

"Will you give me a drink?" Jesus asked the woman at the well.

"You are a Jew and I am a Samaritan woman," she replied. "How can you ask me for a drink?" (John 4:7-9). She was dumbfounded because Jews didn't normally associate with Samaritans, but Jesus welcomed everyone without showing partiality. He didn't cater to the rich, but He didn't associate only with outcasts either. He welcomed Nicodemus, a wealthy religious leader, as well as this sinful Samaritan woman.

The Bible commands us, "Accept one another, then, just as Christ accepted you, in order to bring praise to God" (Romans 15:7). The body of Christ is called to be inclusive just as Jesus was. We are to welcome people from every segment of society. When someone of a different race sits beside you in the pew, what is your reaction? Do you scoot down a little farther, ignore her, look the other way, or greet her warmly? When someone comes into your Sunday school class who is not as polished or well dressed as the rest, how do you respond? Or suppose someone comes in who is obviously wealthy and most in your congregation are not. Do you make him feel comfortable or immediately assume he thinks he's better than the rest of you?

Perhaps you come from a different background than most in this culture. Maybe you're from a minority race or a different socioeconomic status, or you had a rough past. You can help bring unity to the body of Christ by being patient with others, not being easily offended, and forgiving those who have wronged you.

African-American hero Booker T. Washington was the founder and president of Tuskegee Institute in Alabama. He was a gracious, wise leader. Once when he was walking to the school, an elderly woman who didn't know him called to him from her yard: "Hey, boy, would you chop some firewood for me?" Without a word of protest or indignation, Washington stopped, took off his suit coat, chopped some firewood, and even carried some inside for the woman.

After he left, the wealthy woman's maid said, "Ma'am, didn't you know who that was? That was Booker T. Washington, the president of the college." The woman was aghast. She dressed and made her way to the school. She went into the president's office and apologized to Mr. Washington. "I didn't know who you were," she tried to explain.

Though her actions had been appalling, Washington replied graciously. He said, "That's all right, ma'am. I'm always glad to do a favor for a friend." It is said that she became one of the school's most generous supporters.

Some might protest that Washington was being an Uncle Tom or cowardly. I don't think so. I think he was being Christlike, overlooking an offense in an effort to bring racial harmony.

Jesus Told the Truth

"If you knew who I was," Jesus told the woman, "you would be asking me for a drink."

"How can you give me a drink?" she replied. "You have nothing to draw with."

"Drink the water I give you and you will never thirst again," Jesus answered.

"I'll take some of that!" the woman said. "How great it would be not to have to come here to draw water all the time!"

Jesus said, "Go get your husband and come back."

The woman looked away. "I have no husband," she muttered.

"That's right," Jesus said. "You've had five husbands and you're not married to the guy you're living with now."

That wasn't exactly the most tolerant thing Jesus could have said, but the woman wasn't too offended yet. "Sir," she said, "You're obviously a prophet. . . ." She groped for a way to deflect the conversation onto something besides her own sinful life. "My family has always been faithful Samaritans. We worship on this mountain. You Jews say we have to go to the temple."

Here was Jesus' chance to practice tolerance. "Hey, that's OK. You worship God in your own way," Jesus could have said. But He didn't say that because it wouldn't have been true. And it's never loving or right to hide the truth in the name of tolerance. Instead, Jesus said, "You are worshiping what you do not know; we are worshiping what we do know because salvation is from the Jews. But there's something more important. The time is coming very soon when the true worshipers will worship not here nor there but in spirit and in truth."

The beleaguered woman tried a diplomatic response. "Well, I suppose we'll figure it out someday," she said, "when Messiah comes."

Jesus captured her gaze and boldly told the truth: "I am He." The woman was so overcome with emotion that she left her water jug at the well and ran back to town to tell the townspeople what she had witnessed. "Come and see a man who told me the truth about everything in my life," she said. "And He talked to me anyway!"

Jesus didn't just practice tolerance. He practiced truth too. He didn't say it was OK that she was living with her boyfriend. He didn't say worshiping in the temple at Mt. Gerazim was just as good as worshiping in Jerusalem. And He didn't say there were many saviors or Messiahs. He said, "I am He."

Genuine Christian love often dictates that tolerance is not enough. On the Fourth of July weekend a few years ago, I watched from a distance as a babysitter allowed a twelve-year-old and a four-year-old to play with fireworks. Not little firecrackers, but rockets that would shoot several hundred feet in the air and report. The children would light them and walk away, and if the rockets didn't ignite properly, the kids would return to examine them. Several of us in the restaurant who were looking out the window were nervous, fearing that at any moment a child was going to lose an arm or an eye. The babysitter was being tolerant, but she wasn't being loving. She was either ignorant of the danger of the activity or she just didn't care. Those who want us to stand by and be tolerant of others' sinful activity as if it doesn't matter are either ignorant of the danger or they simply don't care. Someone said, "Truth without love is dogmatism. Love without truth is sentimentality. Speaking the truth in love is Christianity."

Some Practical Suggestions

In his book *Christ Above All*, Bob Shannon tells of a time when the Duke of Wellington visited an Anglican church. Everyone in the area was geared up for the visit from such an important dignitary. At the designated time for Communion, the people went forward row by row to receive the elements. When the Duke of Wellington and his entourage went forward and knelt before the altar, every eye was on him. To the horror of the congregation, the back doors suddenly swung open and the town drunk staggered in. He came straight down the aisle and knelt beside the monarch. A quick-thinking usher responded to the scene. He tapped the man on the shoulder and whispered, "Sir, you're going to have to leave. This is the Duke of Wellington."

But the Duke placed his hand on the drunk's shoulder and said, "Stay where you are. There are no dukes here."[3]

The Bible says, "Live in harmony with one another. Do not be proud, but be willing to associate with people of low position. Do not be conceited" (Romans 12:16). Pride and intolerance alienate us from one another. Tolerance and humility breed love and harmony. Let me suggest some practical things you can do in your own life to defeat intolerance and build bridges.

Compare Yourself to Jesus, Not Others

Jesus told a parable about a Pharisee and a tax collector who came to the temple on the same day to pray. The Pharisee proudly thanked God that he was not like the sinful tax collector. Meanwhile the tax collector wept before God and repented of his sins. Jesus said, "I tell you that this man, rather than the other, went home justified before God. For everyone who exalts himself will be humbled, and he who humbles himself will be exalted" (Luke 18:14).

The more you know the perfect man Jesus Christ, the more humble and unworthy you feel. Instead of feeling superior to others, you sense that we are all sinners in need of salvation.

Stand for Your Convictions with a Gentle Spirit

Paul called it "speaking the truth in love" (Ephesians 4:15). If we tolerate one another unconditionally, if we never have the courage to speak the truth, then we will soon be forced to water down the gospel and ultimately lose respect for one another. At the other extreme, if we speak the truth with a clenched fist, then we will offend and alienate others and unnecessarily divide the body of Christ.

Olin Hay was a great old preacher whom I respected very much when he was alive. A doctrinal purist once asked him, "Do you think people who were only sprinkled for baptism will be saved?" He responded, "I hope so! But let me tell you what I understand the Bible to say about baptism." His tone built bridges and won converts much more than that of the angry dogmatist.

Leonardo da Vinci said, "He who knows has no occasion to shout." The Bible says, "Always be prepared to give an answer to everyone who asks you to give the reason for the hope that you have. But do this with gentleness and respect" (1 Peter 3:15).

Reach Out in Friendship to the Person with Whom You Disagree

I am strongly pro-life, but every Thanksgiving I spend several hours with one of my wife's relatives who is strongly pro-abortion. I couldn't disagree with her more. And it's an emotional issue for me. I have a hard time not judging the motives and morals of those who are pro-abortion. At a recent Thanksgiving gathering, I arrived late and walked up to the table of twenty-five people only to discover that the remaining seat was right next to her. We didn't talk about abortion. We talked mostly about our families. When she talked about her son who had died in his twenties a few years earlier, tears streamed from her eyes. I couldn't disagree more strongly with her pro-abortion stance, but I learned that not everyone who disagrees with me is an ogre.

It's one thing to exchange heated letters or make accusations about others, but it's usually a different atmosphere when you have the opportunity to discuss things face-to-face. That's why you're usually wiser to discuss delicate matters with someone in person, one-on-one. Sometimes the issue doesn't need to be confronted again. You both know you have different opinions and are not likely to persuade the other to change his any time soon. Reach out in friendship to the one who disagrees. Two mature people ought to be able to get along with each other even when there are strong disagreements.

Listen Patiently to Those Who Are Different Than You

Several times the Bible mentions the phrase, "The Lord listened. . . ." God is a good listener. Though He never changes His position on truth—in Him there is no "shadow of turning"

(James 1:17, *KJV*)—He listens. If you want to be like God, learn to be a good listener.

As I have grown in my leadership skills, I've had to learn that there is a difference between the way men and women respond in a meeting. When a man nods his head, he usually means, "I agree with you." When a woman nods her head, it means, "I'm listening to you. I understand what you are saying." She may totally disagree, but at least she's listening! Women understand that just because you are listening to someone doesn't mean you have to agree with him. When you carefully, respectfully listen to the person who disagrees with you, you gain an understanding of his position and it is easier to be tolerant. He's also more likely to respectfully listen to you and consider your position.

Let's say you have a grown child who has moved in with his girlfriend. As a Christian, you don't think they should live together without marriage. When you hear the news, you could respond bitterly and say, "Don't think you can bring that girl in this house. We can't risk having other people think we approve of your adultery. We can't approve of that kind of lifestyle." You've made your point, and you've probably made an enemy.

Things would go so much better if you said, "Tell me about your relationship with your girlfriend," and then just listened. After it's all out, you can say, "I can see why you like this girl so much. She seems very special. And I can understand why you're apprehensive about marriage. I don't want you to make a mistake either. Please know that I care about you and love you and want the best for you. I happen to think that what would be best and what God wants for you is to stay celibate or get married. But you're a grown person and you have to make your own decisions. However, this puts me in an awkward situation. When you come here and stay overnight in my house, it sets a bad example for your younger siblings, and it appears to others that I am endorsing your behavior. What would you recommend we do?"

You're not backing down from your convictions, but by talking face-to-face, speaking with gentleness, and listening to his side, you're enhancing the possibility that your relationship will survive and increasing your chances of winning your child to your side.

Practice Seeing People the Way God Sees Them

When Samuel was looking for someone to anoint as King of Israel, he was swayed by the strong appearance and good looks of David's older brother. *Surely, this is to be the Lord's anointed,* Samuel thought. But God told Samuel, "Do not consider his appearance or his height, for I have rejected him. The LORD does not look at the things man looks at. Man looks at the outward appearance, but the LORD looks at the heart" (1 Samuel 16:7). Learn to get beyond the externals and see people for who they are on the inside.

Several years ago, a preacher friend of mine told me about a lesson in tolerance he learned at a Christian service camp. He pulled into the camp around dinnertime on the first night of the week that he was to be a staff member. When he got out of his car, a very unattractive teenage girl he remembered faintly from the previous year came running up to his car. She was thin and stoop-shouldered, with buckteeth and stringy hair. She said self-consciously, "I hope I'm on your team!" He thought to himself, *I hope you're not.*

He quickly unloaded his things and was late arriving for supper. The only seat left in the cafeteria was right across the table from that homely girl. Everyone else had avoided her. They stumbled through awkward conversation until the end of mealtime. The dean of the camp stood up and said, "Since we're so overcrowded this week, please keep the same seat at each meal." *Oh no!* my friend thought, *I've got to go through this three times a day!* He dreaded the rest of the week.

Later, he reflected on that week, saying, "When that girl finally relaxed and I was finally mature enough to listen to her, I discovered that inside that unattractive exterior was one of the deepest, most spiritual teenagers I'd ever met. On Saturday, when I was packing my car to leave, she ran over to the car and through tears thanked me for being her friend. She hugged me and gave me a kiss on the cheek. If she had done that at the beginning of the week, I would have been repulsed. But that kiss made my week." As he drove home, he felt so gratified that he had learned to look at a person not as man does, but as God does.

When Jesus saw the woman at the well, He didn't look at her as man sees her. He didn't see a lowly sinful woman from a despised race. He saw her heart. His tolerant spirit combined with a strong stance for truth saved her soul, and perhaps those of her fellow townspeople. He set an example that we all should follow. By the way, He's tolerant of your sins too. He accepts you and loves you anyway, and He calls you to do the same for others.

3

Serve One Another

I once got up to preach on John 13 and started the message by saying:

> We're going to conclude today's sermon in an unusual way. The message this morning is about Jesus washing the feet of His disciples. When Jesus finished, He said, "As I have washed your feet, so you ought to wash one another's feet." So today we're going to put that command into practice. We can't have a bucket of water and a towel for everybody—that would be physically impossible. But we've secured a number of wet towels and some heavy-duty paper towels that will serve our purpose. At the conclusion of the sermon, the ushers will distribute those items, you will remove your shoes and socks, and we'll wash and dry the feet of the person on our right as a symbol of humility and servanthood.

One guy who was visiting for just the second time nudged his wife and said, "If he's serious, I'm out of here!" I went on to say that we weren't really going to have a foot-washing service. A nervous laughter and collective sigh of relief swept through the congregation, but I had their attention!

I then asked, "Why does the idea make us so uncomfortable?" Maybe we'd be embarrassed for visitors. It's not our custom like it was for people in the New Testament. They wore sandals and walked on dusty roads. When they entered a home, there was a basin of water provided at the door so people could have their feet washed. It was as normal as a host today taking off a guest's coat and hanging it in a hall closet. Since it's not our custom, it would be rude to ask a stranger in our worship service to wash someone else's feet.

Most of us would object, however, because of our own pride. We're either repulsed by the idea of washing someone else's feet—it's beneath our dignity—or we're embarrassed by the thought of someone washing our feet. "I don't want anyone seeing or touching my feet," most of us would say. "My feet are so unattractive." "I've got a damaged toenail." "I've got corns." "I've got these ugly bunions."

Our pride not only keeps us from foot-washing services, but more importantly, it keeps us from doing practical acts of service every day. Our sophistication sometimes prohibits us from representing Christ to the world. I hope this chapter will help break down that pride and motivate you to be willing to serve others. "Now that I, your Lord and Teacher, have washed your feet, you also should wash one another's feet," Jesus said. "I have set you an example that you should do as I have done for you" (John 13:14, 15).

The Example of Jesus

John introduces the account by explaining:

> It was just before the Passover Feast. Jesus knew that the time had come for him to leave this world and go to the Father. Having loved his own who were in the world, he now showed them the full extent of his love. The evening meal was being served (John 13:1, 2).

The host would normally provide not only a basin of water but also a servant at the door so that the guests could have their feet cleaned before entering the house. Not only were their feet dirty from walking with open shoes on dusty roads, they also customarily reclined at the table when they ate, so their feet were almost at the elbow of the person beside them, not hidden under the table. Feet were visible and *smellable*, so it was important that they be clean. A person would usually give even more attention to washing his feet before a meal than we do our hands. If a host wasn't available, like in this particular instance, then the first ones in the room would usually make provisions for the washing of people's feet much as we might turn on the lights and set up the chairs. When no host or servant was available, someone would volunteer to take the role of the servant and do the foot washing. But on this night—the night before Jesus was to go to the cross—not one disciple stooped to take the servant's role.

The Disciples' Prideful Inattention

The Gospel of Luke gives us insight into why nobody offered to wash feet that night. They were bickering about who among them was the greatest (22:24). Can you believe that? On Jesus' last night with them, they were arguing over who was most important! This was no quiet discussion either.

How disappointed Jesus must have been at their pride. In their minds, for one of them to stoop to the servant's task would be paramount to giving up their claim to greatness among the twelve. They were all too important for such a menial task. They all fought over the throne. No one fought over the towel.

That was so dumb. The disciples had no basis for pride. They were nobodies—common fishermen, ignorant Galileans. If it hadn't been for Jesus' selection, nobody would have ever heard of Simon Peter, James, or John. But a little recognition had gone to their heads and they had lost perspective.

We do the same thing, though. Only through our association

with Christ do we have any worth. Apart from Him we're nobody—just dust—but we brag about our accomplishments, our finances, our education. Someone asked Albert Einstein how much of all the knowledge in the world he possessed. He said one tenth of one percent. Maybe he really thought he was being humble, but today we know he grossly overestimated his own intelligence. Imagine how the God of the universe laughs at our exaggerated estimation of our own importance.

Jesus' Genuine Motivation

Jesus was the victim of gross neglect. He was the honored guest, and it was His last night with the disciples. However, no one offered to wash His feet. Nobody seemed to even notice the oversight. Most of us would have felt sorry for ourselves and had a pity party or thrown a fit. Jesus responded differently.

I think at least two sincere motivations prompted Jesus to take on the role of servant himself.

He had compassion for His disciples. The biblical account begins, "Having loved his own . . ." (John 13:1). Even though they had neglected Him and would fail Him, Jesus still loved them. A genuine servant is a person who is motivated by love for others, who loves so much that he becomes more concerned about the others' welfare than his own.

Jesus was motivated by His confidence in His mission. "Jesus knew that the Father had put all things under his power, and that he had come from God and was returning to God; so he got up from the meal, took off his outer clothing, and wrapped a towel around his waist" (John 13:3, 4). Jesus was self-assured. He knew exactly who He was and why He had come into the world. He had come to serve the world by being its Savior, to give himself as a ransom for many. He had a sense of purpose that would not be deterred by petty disagreements or temporary pain.

A servant is humble but not insecure. A servant is self-sacrificing but not self-conscious. People who lack self-confidence seldom serve well. They fear rejection and humiliation, and they hide instead of serving. One preacher said, "Humility is not thinking less of yourself. Humility is not thinking of yourself at all." In spite of the pressures around Him, Jesus wasn't thinking primarily of himself. He was thinking of His disciples. He took the opportunity to teach them one final lesson about who He was and who He expected them to be.

Jesus' Humble Demonstration

Jesus got up, took off His robe, and wrapped himself in a towel. "After that, he poured water into a basin and began to wash his disciples' feet, drying them with the towel that was wrapped around him" (John 13:5).

This was *inconvenient* for Jesus. When we sit down at a meal, we don't like to get back up to get something. We certainly wouldn't like the idea of getting up to perform someone else's time-consuming chore. But Jesus interrupted His meal to perform this menial task.

It was also *undignified*. He took off His outer garment lest His clothing get soaked. He bared His chest and legs, knelt down on the hard floor, and began to wash twenty-four dirty feet. That's not very dignified for the most powerful man who ever walked the earth.

And it was *unsanitary*. He was about to eat and now He had to touch dirty, smelly feet. Some of them must have had rashes, corns, warts, and fungus. He washed and dried them while the disciples sat there dumbfounded. He didn't wear rubber gloves to protect himself from disease. He touched their feet. That's not very sanitary.

It was also *unfair*. John mentions a footnote in his introduction to the story: "The devil had already prompted Judas Iscariot, son of Simon, to betray Jesus" (13:2). Judas was there even though he had already made arrangements to sell Jesus out. Judas didn't leave until later in the evening, yet Jesus washed his feet, too.

I'd love to see an artist's rendition of Jesus stooping low to wash the feet of the man He knew had already betrayed Him.

What an example of grace! Charles Swindoll said if he'd been Jesus, he would have filled a tub with boiling water and said, "Stick your feet in there, Bubba. That will clean you up! You need to get accustomed to some heat!" But Jesus didn't just serve those who appreciated Him or agreed with Him. He knelt low and served the one who was about to sell Him out.

Peter's Self-Righteous Objection

As Jesus made His way down the line, the disciples must have been shocked and humiliated. The one who should have been the guest of honor was doing the work of a slave. Peter couldn't keep his mouth shut. When it was his turn to have his feet washed, he strongly objected: "Lord, are you going to wash my feet?" (John 13:6). In the Greek text, the two pronouns are side by side: "You—Mine?"

Jesus replied, "You do not realize now what I am doing, but later you will understand."

"No," said Peter, "you shall never wash my feet" (John 13:7, 8). The Greek is emphatic: "No, never!" Not until eternity will you wash my feet!

At first glance it appears that Peter is really humble. "After all, Lord," he seems to be saying, "I should be washing your feet." But that's not what he had in mind. This is self-assertive pride. There is a pride that refuses anyone's assistance:

- I can handle my problems myself—I don't need a counselor.
- I would never lower myself to ask for financial assistance.
- I can find it myself. I don't need to stop and ask directions!
- I'll wash my own feet, Jesus.

When you serve others, it may surprise you when some people object. You may think that if you're serving people, everyone will be pleased with you; however, that's not usually the case. "We don't need your help," someone will say. "Who do you think you are? Are you trying to make the rest of us look bad?"

A minister who worked in the inner city told me how he and a group of men rented out a vacant church building and began a program for inner-city youth. They had discovered that lots of young children had nothing to do after school because their mothers were working, and so the kids were just roaming the streets. The men developed a volunteer program and invited the kids inside to play games, have something to eat, and hear a Bible story. One day a woman approached the minister and said, "Are you in charge of this after-school program?"

"Yes," he said.

"My son is in your program," she said.

"What's his name?" the minister asked. When she told him, he replied, "Oh, your son is a fine boy!"

"Well, that's what I'm here to talk to you about," she said. "I don't want you telling him any more of those Bible stories. You can feed him and he can play, but no more stories."

"Why?" he asked.

"You're giving him the idea that he's just as good as anybody else, and you're setting him up to get hurt," she reasoned. The minister gently explained that Bible stories were part of the deal, and he hoped she would reconsider, but he knew there was a chance the boy may never come back.

When you wash feet, brace yourself for some criticism—no matter how noble your motives may be.

Jesus answered Peter's objection: "Unless I wash you, you have no part with me."

"Then, Lord," Simon Peter replied, "not just my feet but my hands and my head as well!" (John 13:8, 9).

Charles Swindoll said, "Peter was the kind of guy who, when he got the truth, he hung himself with it. Once he caught on, he went all the way to the extreme." I can imagine Thomas shaking his head in disgust, and James and John rolling their eyes with impatience.

Jesus told Peter, "A person who has had a bath needs only to wash his feet; his whole body is clean. And you are clean, though not every one of you" (John 13:10). The act Jesus was performing had both a physical and spiritual purpose. He wasn't just washing their feet; He was teaching them something about service and how much He loved them. So when Jesus said, "Peter, your body is clean; only your feet are dirty," He meant something spiritual—Peter was clean on the inside, too. But not all of them were clean on the inside, Jesus said. In the next verse, John explains, "For he knew who was going to betray him, and that was why he said not every one was clean" (13:11).

Jesus' Challenging Instructions

When He was finished, Jesus sat back down at the table and explained the importance of what had just happened. "Do you understand what I have done for you?" He asked them. "You call me 'Teacher' and 'Lord,' and rightly so, for that is what I am" (John 13:12, 13). Jesus didn't have pseudo humility. He didn't say, "I'm on the same level with all you guys. We're just all pals. We're coleaders." He didn't refuse to be considered a leader. He knew He was their Teacher and Lord.

"Now that I, your Lord and Teacher, have washed your feet," He continued, "you also should wash one another's feet" (John 13:14). You would have expected Him to say, "Now that I've washed your feet, you need to wash my feet." That would be great! We would be anxious to wash the feet of our Lord. Instead, He said, "You wash *one another's* feet." That's a different matter! Serving the Lord is a delight. Serving each other can often be drudgery. Jesus concluded:

> I have set you an example that you should do as I have done for you. I tell you the truth, no servant is greater than his master, nor is a messenger greater than the one who sent him. Now that you know these things, you will be blessed if you do them (John 13:15-17).

I don't think Jesus intended to establish foot washing as an ordinance like the Lord's Supper, to be practiced during weekly worship. We don't read of the New Testament Christians practicing foot washing in their worship services. When Jesus said, "Do as I have done," He didn't mean we should duplicate the act of foot washing. He was saying we should observe the principle: "As I have served you, so you should serve one another."

The Lessons for Us

Can you grasp how radical a lifestyle Jesus is calling us to? He not only saves you from your sins, He wants to save you from the futile lifestyle of the world around you. The Christian is to live counterculture.

The World Defers to the Proud, But God Honors the Humble

The world emphasizes building up self-esteem, standing up for your rights, getting what you deserve, and even dying with dignity. Jesus Christ urges you to crucify yourself, surrender your rights, submit to the authorities, and humble yourself before God.

The world honors the powerful, the rich, and the famous. God honors the bent knee, broken heart, and wet eye. God doesn't save the strutter; He saves the humble. He doesn't use superstars; He uses servants. Jesus himself set the example for us by spending His first day on earth in a manger and the last day before His death washing the feet of some lowly fishermen. The Scripture reminds us several times, "God opposes the proud but gives grace to the humble" (James 4:6).

Chuck Colson is one of the most brilliant and capable leaders in America today. His education in law and political science combined with his experience as special advisor to President Nixon have qualified him to speak to influential and powerful people. In the seventies, he was sent to prison for Watergate crimes. A proud man was humbled. A powerful man had to answer to prison guards. But Charles Colson dedicated his life to Jesus Christ and now spends his time ministering primarily to prisoners, not politicians.

Though he leads thousands of volunteers in his Prison Fellowship ministry, Colson still visits prisons himself and speaks often in prison chapels. I've accompanied him to prisons and watched him speak respectfully to the prisoners. "Hi, I'm Chuck Colson," he will say. "How long have you been here? Are they treating you right? Do you know the Lord?" There's no apology, not much small talk, no embarrassment. He gets right to the heart of the matter. And he is effective in leading prisoners to Christ.

I've walked across prison grounds with him and heard prisoners call out, "Hi, Chuck!" I smile, because I know that only inside prison walls is he *not* referred to as Mr. Colson or Dr. Colson. He genuinely loves going into the places where he is just "Chuck, the ex-con." Here's Chuck Colson, who more than almost anyone in the country is qualified to speak to presidents and intellectuals about Christ, but God is using him primarily as a servant to prisoners and inmates. God took Chuck's greatest humiliation and used it to the glory of Jesus Christ.

The World Respects Status, but God Rewards Service

We are drilled from almost every angle to be conscious of our status. The education system urges you to study hard and get good grades so you can graduate with honors and display your degree. The business world rewards those who succeed by giving them titles, perks, and bonuses. If you want to be considered important in the world, you have to sit in the nicest seats at concerts and ball games, drive the finest cars, and live in the plushest neighborhoods.

Jesus calls us to forget status and pursue servanthood. The Pharisees were status-conscious, and Jesus said of them:

> Everything they do is done for men to see: They make
> their phylacteries wide and the tassels on their garments
> long; they love the place of honor at banquets and the

most important seats in the synagogues; they love to be greeted in the marketplaces and to have men call them "Rabbi" (Matthew 23:5-7).

Jesus said not to be like them. "The greatest among you will be your servant," He promised. "For whoever exalts himself will be humbled, and whoever humbles himself will be exalted" (Matthew 23:11, 12). God exalts doctors who don't insist on titles, brilliant educators who communicate in normal vocabulary, powerful politicians who are sensitive to the common man, attractive people who don't manipulate, great athletes who don't strut, rich people who don't flaunt it, and average people who aren't envious of those who have more. That's so different from the way the world measures worth, but God's ways are not our ways, and His thoughts are not our thoughts.

Where are you serving? Jesus said, "As I have washed your feet, so you ought also to wash one another's feet." Jesus saw the need and responded to it. Nobody assigned Him the title "Senior Vice President in Charge of Foot Washing." He just did it because there was a need. You don't need someone assigning you a task. Just look for a need and start filling it.

You can start by serving in little ways. In your home, think of the other family members ahead of yourself. Pick up your clothes so your mother doesn't have to. Help your brother or sister with a chore. Turn off the ball game and listen to your wife. Help get the children ready for bed. Fix your husband's favorite meal again.

When you go to church, park at the back of the lot so the older people can have the better parking spots. Help the single mom carry her diaper bags into the building. Help pick up bulletins when the service is over.

At work, give a hand to someone in another department. Relieve a coworker by doing a menial task for someone who is subordinate to you. Change the water jug. Fix the coffee.

And if you really want a special reward from God, serve anonymously! It will be so difficult to do an act of service and not let *anyone* but God know you did it, but what growth you will experience. And you will make somebody's day.

Philosopher Thomas La Mance said that as a boy he was lounging around in the living room listening to the radio when his dad came in from shoveling snow:

> My dad looked at me quizzically and said, "By tomorrow you won't even remember what you were listening to. How about doing something for the next twenty minutes that you will remember for the next twenty years! I promise that you will enjoy it every time you think of it."
>
> "What is it?" I asked.
>
> "Well, son, there are several inches of snow on old Mrs. Brown's walk," my dad said. "Why don't you see if you can shovel it off and get back home without her knowing?"
>
> I did the walk in about fifteen minutes. She never knew who did the job, and Dad was right. It has been a lot more than twenty years and I have enjoyed the memory every time I have thought about it.[4]

That may sound simple, but it's not easy to put into practice. It means you have to go against your own carnal nature that is driving you to be lazy and egotistical. It means you must go counter to the world around you telling you to be proud and egocentric. And it means you must be willing to be taken advantage of, taken for granted, and abused. Jesus said, "I tell you the truth, no servant is greater than his master, nor is a messenger greater than the one who sent him" (John 13:16). Jesus was taken advantage of, yet He served.

The World Pursues Happiness, But God Promises Blessedness

"Now that you know these things," Jesus said, "you will be blessed if you do them" (John 13:17).

The world tries unsuccessfully to be happy by indulging in selfish pursuits. Jesus said, "If you become a servant, you will be blessed." A recent *Reader's Digest* article reported on a study proving that elderly people who regularly do small acts of kindness for others live much longer than those who are more self-centered. The study showed that even one small act of kindness will lengthen someone's life![5]

Dr. Karl Menninger, noted Christian psychologist, was once asked what you should do if you feel a period of depression coming on. You'd expect the doctor to prescribe a vacation or at least a brief period of rest. He said, "If I felt a sense of futility overwhelming me, I'd go out of my house, lock the door, go across the tracks and find someone in need, and do whatever I could to assist that person." In other words, sound mental health is contingent upon ministering to others. We are happiest when our lives have a purpose, and we find that purpose by serving others in need.

Dr. Dan Garcia of our church wrote an article in a local medical journal a few years ago about the joy he experienced from participating in short-term missions. He wrote:

> A newly found joy for me is one that I've also been able to share with my wife Rita. No, I'm not talking about a new hobby or a new possession or vacation, but the opportunity to practice medicine in a missionary setting on a short-term basis.
>
> Through the coordinated efforts of Southeast Christian Church and a team of permanent missionaries located in rural Jamaica, my wife and I [have participated in several short-term trips]. Our trips have been experiences we will forever cherish. . . . The fulfillment of spending our vacations with such singleness of purpose was truly a joy. The opportunity to compare our busy American lifestyle to a simpler, less hectic and slower paced lifestyle was an eye-opener. But the chance to truly discern what it means to have a servant's heart in less than desirable conditions was probably the most uplifting part of our whole experience.
>
> . . . It was exciting, quite hot, sometimes frustrating and heart wrenching to see the deplorable and unimaginable conditions of the poor and the lonely. . . . But as for Rita and me, a message that we learned repeatedly from our

brief missionary experience was that no action is too small for the Lord, and anything done in and for and through him is a great success.

. . . Our lives are a bit different now. No lightning bolt experience here, but we have renewed and more purposeful goals in our lives. And as a result we have a newly found joy to add to our list of other blessings.[6]

Jesus said, "Whoever wants to save his life will lose it, but whoever loses his life for me will find it" (Matthew 16:25), and "It is more blessed to give than to receive" (Acts 20:35). The world pursues happiness and can't find it. The Christian pursues servanthood and finds ultimate fulfillment.

4

Comfort One Another

I love my job, but one of the downsides is facing so much tragedy and grief every week. If you were to try to think of the worst thing that could possibly happen to a person—that which would bring about the greatest amount of grief—what would it be? One of your children is killed? You discover your spouse has been unfaithful? Both of your parents die unexpectedly? You're told you have a terminal illness in your youth? You're financially bankrupt? Your mate is shipped off to war? Different members of our congregation have recently experienced each one of these scenarios.

When I first entered the ministry, an old preacher advised me, "Son, every time you preach, remember that there is at least one broken heart in every pew." I've discovered that he underestimated it. On any given weekend when I stand up to preach, I know that many in our congregation are suffering from grief and need to be comforted.

Grief is the prolonged, life-shaking sorrow someone experiences after a significant loss. Sometimes grief is right on the surface and evident in flowing tears. At other times it hides behind a person's activity, fake smiles, and phony conversations. Grief is still there, however, even when it is unseen.

When C. S. Lewis's wife died, he wrote, "Her absence is like the sky, spread over everything."[7]

Grief is not only something we experience at the death of a loved one. It is the emotion or combination of emotions we experience when we lose anyone or anything we care about deeply. Some people grieve the loss of a loved one who is still alive. Perhaps a child is leaving the house and going off to college, or a parent is slipping away mentally with Alzheimer's disease, and grief comes. Adult children whose parents are going through a divorce often grieve over the family structure and support that is now gone. The amputee who loses an arm or leg grieves. People who move after developing deep roots in a community grieve the loss of relationships. A young man may grieve when his romance breaks up. A wife whose husband abandons her grieves the loss of protection and provision. Whenever we lose any person or possession that has provided emotional security or satisfaction, grief may follow.

Peter warned that until Heaven comes, for a little while we might have to "suffer grief in all kinds of trials" (1 Peter 1:6). Jesus promised, "Blessed are those who mourn, for they will be comforted" (Matthew 5:4). The Bible challenges us to be God's instruments, comforting one another with the comfort we ourselves received from God:

> Praise be to the God and Father of our Lord Jesus Christ, the Father of compassion and the God of all comfort, who comforts us in all our troubles, so that we can comfort those in any trouble with the comfort we ourselves have received from God. For just as the sufferings of Christ flow over into our lives, so also through Christ our comfort overflows. If we are distressed, it is for your comfort and salvation; if we are comforted, it is for your comfort, which produces in you patient endurance of the same sufferings we suffer. And our hope for you is firm, because we know that just as you share in our sufferings, so also you share in our comfort (2 Corinthians 1:3-7).

In John 11 there is a thrilling account of how Jesus brought comfort and hope to two sisters who were grieving over the death of their brother. While the cause of their grief was the death of a loved one, the lessons we learn from Jesus will help us comfort the grieving no matter what the cause may be. If you're not grieving right now, pay attention to the lessons in this chapter because God may be calling you to comfort someone else who is grieving. And someday you will need to be comforted by another.

The Death of Lazarus

The story begins with the death of Lazarus, a close friend of Jesus.

> So the sisters sent word to Jesus, "Lord, the one you love is sick."
> When he heard this, Jesus said, "This sickness will not end in death. No, it is for God's glory so that God's Son may be glorified through it." Jesus loved Martha and her sister and Lazarus. Yet when he heard that Lazarus was sick, he stayed where he was two more days (John 11:3-6).

Why did Jesus wait two days before responding when He heard Lazarus was ill? Lazarus was a close friend, so you'd expect Jesus to drop everything and rush to his side. He'd opened the eyes of the blind; surely He could heal His sick friend. I think there are at least two reasons Jesus waited.

Lazarus was already dead. By the time Jesus received the news, Lazarus had already died. Jesus was at Betharba, twenty miles from Bethany, when He first received the news. He could have made the trip to Bethany in one day. He waited two days and then made the day's journey. When He arrived, Lazarus had been dead for four days. So Lazarus apparently died the very day the messengers left to contact Jesus. By the time they arrived, they didn't know Lazarus had already died, but Jesus knew because He is God. Jesus knew He wasn't going to prevent death or grief by going right away.

Jesus waited that God might be glorified. Jesus said, "This sickness will not end in death" (John 11:2). Later He told His disciples that Lazarus had already died (John 11:14), so He obviously knew Lazarus was dead. But He said it wouldn't *end* in death. There's going to be another chapter in Lazarus's story. "It is for God's glory," Jesus added, "so that God's Son may be glorified through it" (John 11:4). To resurrect someone after he has been dead four days is a spectacular miracle. The fact that it had been four days would have been significant to some of the Jews who had a superstition that the soul stayed around the body for three days in hopes of returning. So for Jesus to raise Lazarus after four days would convince both the skeptic and the superstitious that a miracle had really been performed, and God would get the glory.

Jesus told His disciples, "Lazarus is dead, and for your sake I am glad I was not there, so that you may believe. But let us go to him" (John 11:14, 15).

The Grief of Martha and Mary

When Jesus arrived in Bethany, He found Martha and Mary grieving their brother's death.

> On his arrival, Jesus found that Lazarus had already been in the tomb for four days. Bethany was less than two miles from Jerusalem, and many Jews had come to Martha and Mary to comfort them in the loss of their brother (John 11:17-19).

The Bible says there is a time to mourn (Ecclesiastes 3:4). A minister once told me about a young woman in his church who asked him to talk to her grandfather. "He's been so down and irritable lately," she said.

The preacher asked, "Is there anything that you can point to that would contribute to his emotional condition?"

"Well, Grandma died," she said, "but that was six weeks ago. You'd think he'd be over it by now. He's making us all depressed!" She didn't understand the grief process. Grief is a normal experience. Expressing grief is healthy and appropriate when someone you love has died.

If you are going to comfort others, you need to understand some things about grief. It's not over in six weeks or even in six months. Elisabeth Kubler-Ross suggested in her best-seller on grief that there are five stages of grief: denial, anger, bargaining, depression, and acceptance.[8] People don't go through the phases rigidly, leaving one and then abruptly going to the second, but I've observed that there is some general truth to Ross's categories. I think Haddon Robinson's breakdown of the grief process may be even more helpful. In his article, "Grief," he suggests that people go through three primary stages of grief.[9]

The Crisis Stage

The *crisis stage* is the briefest of the three stages, usually lasting just a few days. In the case of the death of a loved one, it lasts from the moment of death till the funeral, or a few days longer if the death was sudden. During this stage the grief sufferer experiences a range of emotions—shock, surprise, denial, disbelief. Even when the death is expected and has finally happened, people may deny it and say, "I can't take it all in." It feels like a bad dream. "Numbness takes place almost as though an anesthesia has been administered," Robinson says.[10] The griever will usually shed many tears, sometimes in the presence of friends, sometimes just alone. Sometimes there is uncontrollable emotion. When ministering to a mother who has just been told her child has died suddenly, I've heard deep inner groanings that are impossible to describe. The Bible mentions this kind of grieving when Herod slaughtered the babies in Bethlehem: "A voice is heard in Ramah, weeping and great mourning, Rachel weeping for her children and refusing to be comforted, because they are no more" (Matthew 2:18).

The Crucible Stage

A crucible is a vessel used for melting substances at a high degree of heat. After the crisis stage, the griever goes through a difficult refining period Robinson calls the *crucible stage*. According to Robinson, this stage is the most intense during the first six to twelve weeks, but can last a long time—up to two years or longer, depending on the closeness of the relationship and the circumstances of the loss. The suddenness of the death, whether it was violent or peaceful, whether the griever was partly responsible, and other circumstances will cause the crucible stage to vary in length.

The grief sufferer is bound by a thousand emotional cords to the person who has been lost. During this period, the mourner must slowly break the emotional ties with the past and all the future expectations that were at one time bound up with the person who is gone.

Six months after my father died, I was watching the Pittsburgh Steelers play football on television. My dad was a big Steelers fan. When they won, I thought, *I ought to call my dad*. Then I remembered—he's not here anymore. I can't call him. Years later I would still say, "I need to go up to Mom and Dad's this summer to visit." That's how my grief affects me. How much more intense it must be for my mother who was married to him for over fifty years.

During the crucible stage, Robinson says that deep depression can smother an individual so completely that an otherwise emotionally healthy person may begin to feel he's losing his mind.[11]

A person in this stage of grief feels isolated from others because friends who were there for comfort during the crisis stage are returning to their busy routines. Sometimes weeks or even months will go by when suddenly a desperate sense of loneliness and grief overwhelm the griever. Barbara Roberts, former governor of Oregon, wrote a book on grief after her husband died from lung cancer. She suggested that if someone very close to you dies, the most difficult period of time will be seven to nine months after the death. While the world moves on, you realize you still badly miss your loved one and wonder if you will ever get over the feeling of loss.[12]

Feelings of guilt often accompany this stage. People think things like, *I should have done more during that last illness. I should have expressed my love more. I wish I hadn't been so harsh toward her.*

Anger may also rise to the surface. Both Mary and Martha challenged Jesus, "Lord, if you had been here, this wouldn't have happened" (John 11:21, 32). The griever will often feel anger toward friends, the physician, life, death, God, and even the person who died, bursting out, "Why did you go and do this to me, leaving me all alone?"

After the death of his wife, C. S. Lewis wrote about his experience with grief in *A Grief Observed*:

> No one ever told me that grief felt so like fear. I am not afraid, but the sensation is like being afraid. The same fluttering in the stomach, the same restlessness, the yawning. I keep on swallowing. At other times it feels like being mildly drunk or concussed. There is a sort of invisible blanket between the world and me. I find it hard to take in what anyone says. Or perhaps, hard to want to take it in. It is so uninteresting.[13]

Lewis spoke of feelings of laziness, insomnia, exhaustion, and futility. He said he hated the embarrassment of people who didn't know what to say. He grew impatient with people's surface comments and flippant attitudes. He almost published the book under a pseudonym, perhaps because he feared it would seem inappropriate or inconsistent for a man who had boasted of strong faith and had helped others through their doubts to be writing so honestly about his own grief and doubts. Grief is a severe test even for the most mature Christian.

The Construction Stage

Robinson says the final stage is the *construction stage* in which the mourner begins to recreate new patterns for living. Dr. Cyril J. Barber explains:

> And finally, a remarkable thing begins to happen. We notice that for short periods the hurt is not as great. There is a "light at the end of the tunnel" after all. Anniversaries, however, and other special occasions like Christmas and birthdays, et cetera, will still make us reminisce about the past. And there will be tears. But with each reminder there will also come a sense of thankfulness to the Lord for His sustaining grace.[14]

Haddon Robinson wrote,

> People need to be encouraged to move out into activities as soon as they have emotional energy to invest in them. These activities should not be distractions to keep the bereaved from facing grief; instead, they come about as a result of having faced it.[15]

During this time, in order to establish a new, creative pattern for living, a person may find a new job, begin volunteering at church, enroll in college, or take up a new hobby. I've heard Dr. Lewis Foster, retired Cincinnati Bible College professor, talk about viewing life in terms of chapters. There comes a time to close a chapter. That chapter is always there as a part of the book you helped to write and you can go back and review it, but you refuse to live the rest of your life in yesterday's chapter.

Years ago, we started a group for new widows in our church. They called themselves "The Next Chapter." They got together to comfort each other in their grief. We discovered that after several years, the women who started the group were doing such a good job and having so much fun together that they couldn't relate to someone who had just lost her husband. We had to start another group for those who had recently lost a loved one.

It's a healthy sign that the widows in "The Next Chapter" were ready to move on. It is not a tribute to your loved one or to your faith in the God of the future for you to give up and live in the past. There comes a time to move on, to say with the psalmist, "This is the day the LORD has made; [I will] rejoice and be glad in it" (118:24).

The Comfort of Jesus Christ

In the midst of grief, Jesus brought comfort and hope. Notice three things that Jesus did, which we too can do to help bring comfort to the grieving.

He Came to Where They Were

Though the sisters were disappointed that Jesus didn't come sooner, He came nonetheless. He knew He could provide even more comfort after the initial shock of Lazarus's death had worn off, after the crisis had passed.

Jesus' example reminds us that mourners often need their close friends more during the crucible stage than the crisis stage. A friend told me that his second Christmas without his wife was more difficult than the first. His wife had died near Thanksgiving, and during that first Christmas season, many friends watched out for him, keeping him busy and encouraging him. But the next Christmas he was caught off guard. Since it had been over a year since she had died, he felt more confident he could handle things. He didn't plan as many activities to help him deal with his grief, and he was blindsided with memories of past Christmases with his wife. Sitting through the Christmas Eve service at church with his two children by his side was almost more than he could endure.

Sympathy abounds immediately after someone experiences a loss. People flock to the funeral home and send flowers while the family is still numb. However, six weeks or six months later, when the loneliness and loss really make their strongest impression, friends are needed more than ever. You can make the biggest impact in bringing comfort to the grieving if you will remember the griever after most have forgotten.

The Bible says, "A friend loves at all times, and a brother is born for adversity" (Proverbs 17:17). If you want to be a Christian brother to someone, stay by the person throughout his grief. The griever will be comforted when he realizes he's not alone. Be there to meet basic needs. Don't say, "If I can do anything, call me." Look for a need and take care of it. Babysitting, returning phone calls, paying the bills, doing the laundry, cooking meals, writing thank-you notes, and running errands can seem like insurmountable burdens to the griever but are little things you can help take care of.

And listen to him when he wants to talk about the one who died. Sometimes friends don't want to bring up the one who died because they're afraid it will open old wounds. *I don't want to make her cry*, the friend thinks. Mentioning a conversation you had with the one who died or a good memory from the past demonstrates that you, too, miss the person. It can be therapeutic and comforting for the griever to be given the opportunity to talk about the one who has gone.

He Reminded Them of Their Faith

"Your brother will rise again," Jesus said (John 11:23), reminding Martha of her faith. When I was notified that my father had suffered a serious stroke, a minister friend of mine comforted me, prayed with me, and then said, "Now it's time to practice what you preach." His tone wasn't rude but comforting, and I knew it was a reminder that I needed to hear.

Martha answered Jesus, "I know he will rise again in the resurrection at the last day."

Jesus responded, "I am the resurrection and the life. He who believes in me will live, even though he dies; and whoever lives and believes in me will never die. Do you believe this?" (John 11:24-26).

Scottish preacher James Stewart pointed out that Jesus

deliberately placed himself at the center of His message. He didn't say, as other teachers, "The truth is everything; I am nothing." He said, "I am the truth." He didn't claim, as the founders of other religions, to have the answer to the world's enigmas. He claimed to *be* the answer: "I am the way." He didn't speculate about the possibility of life beyond the grave; He avowed, "I am the resurrection and the life. Believe me and you will live." Only Jesus Christ provides the answer to the grieving heart. Jesus pointed the grievers to himself.

Martha responded to Jesus, "Yes, Lord, I believe that you are the Christ, the Son of God, who was to come into the world" (John 11:27). The words Martha said are in the perfect tense in the Greek, indicating a fixed and settled faith. Martha was saying, "I have believed and I will continue to believe that You are the Messiah, even though I don't fully understand right now."

Most of the time, people who are believers don't want or need to hear pious clichés or long discourses about Heaven, but you can gently remind them of the hope that comes only in Jesus Christ.

Once when others were turning away from Jesus, He asked His disciples if they, too, were going to leave Him. Simon Peter answered, "Lord, to whom shall we go? You have the words of eternal life. We believe and know that you are the Holy One of God" (John 6:68).

When the nineteen-year-old grandson of a wonderful Christian man in our church took his own life, his grandfather was devastated. A few days later, I saw the grandfather at church. He grabbed me, hugged me, and whispered, "I've still got my faith." All I could say was, "Hold on to that, Joe." Sometimes your faith is all you have and it's the only thing that sustains you.

Often in grief a person will ask questions about God. "Why did God allow this to happen? Doesn't God care about me? Why didn't He stop it?" Any attempt to answer such questions comes across as shallow and empty. It's usually best to say as little as possible. Sometimes it's enough to simply say, "I'll be praying for you." If the time is right, you can sometimes comfort the griever by saying, "I don't know the answer to your questions. I, too, wonder why God would allow this. But I know God has promised never to leave you. Remember Jesus alone has the words of eternal life. There is no place else to turn. Hold on to your faith."

He Mourned with Them

The Gospels point out the personality differences between these two sisters. Martha was practical and efficient; Mary was emotional and compassionate. Martha came to Jesus standing erect, questioning Him boldly. Mary stayed at home until she was told that Jesus was asking for her, and then she hurried to Him and fell at His feet weeping.

People grieve differently. Couples who lose a child have a very difficult time comforting each other because feelings, expressions, and the timing of going through the stages of grief will differ for them. A mutual grief can actually drive couples apart if they don't have a high degree of understanding and tolerance.

Jesus understood the difference between the sisters and responded accordingly. He answered Martha with Scripture and logic; He responded to Mary with emotion.

> When Jesus saw her weeping, and the Jews who had come along with her also weeping, he was deeply moved in spirit and troubled. "Where have you laid him?" he asked.
> "Come and see, Lord," they replied (John 11:33, 34).

The next verse is one of the most memorized verses in the Bible because it's the shortest! "Jesus wept" (John 11:35).

In our culture, men try to suppress their tears. Any open display of emotion is discouraged as a sign of weakness. "Big boys don't cry," they are told. By the time a boy reaches adolescence, he's convinced that tears and manliness don't go together. By the time he reaches fifty, he may not know how to weep at all.

Women, too, may conceive of weeping as a weakness. Onlookers watch the widow of a dignitary at his funeral and remark, "How brave she is! She didn't shed a tear!" Many people regard courage and tears as enemies without understanding that weeping is a language of the soul. Some even think that if we have faith, we won't be so brokenhearted and tearful.

God created tears partly for the purpose of expressing sorrow. Charles Dickens wrote, "Heaven knows we need never be ashamed of our tears, for they are the rain upon the blinding dust of earth, overlaying our hard hearts."[16]

Those who are too sophisticated to cry are more sophisticated than Jesus. Seeing His tears, Lazarus's friends and family remarked of Jesus, "See how he loved him!" (John 11:36). He who was perfect stood by a graveside and wept.

Why did Jesus weep if He knew He was going to raise Lazarus from the dead? I think it's because He saw Mary weeping and grieved with her. He was reminded how death hurts so many people down through the ages. When one of your parents dies, it breaks your heart to see the other parent hurting so deeply.

Or maybe Jesus was remembering how He grieved when one of His loved ones died. Joseph apparently died while Jesus was young, and perhaps Jesus could remember grieving for His earthly father. Jesus knew the pain that Lazarus's sisters were experiencing and the grief that death would bring people for centuries to come.

One of the ways you bring comfort to those you love is by grieving with them and even weeping with those who weep (Romans 12:15). I love the old story about the little girl who, shortly after her young playmate was tragically killed, went to comfort her friend's mother. When she returned home, her father asked her what she had said to the grieving mother. "Nothing," she replied. "I just climbed up in her lap and cried with her."

The Resurrection of the Dead

Jesus did a fourth thing to bring comfort to Mary and Martha—something only God can do: He raised Lazarus from the dead.

> Jesus, once more deeply moved, came to the tomb. It was a cave with a stone laid across the entrance. "Take away the stone," he said.
>
> "But, Lord," said Martha, the sister of the dead man, "by this time there is a bad odor, for he has been there four days."
>
> Then Jesus said, "Did I not tell you that if you believed, you would see the glory of God?"
>
> So they took away the stone. Then Jesus looked up and said, "Father, I thank you that you have heard me. I knew that you always hear me, but I said this for the benefit of the people standing here, that they may believe that you sent me."
>
> When he had said this, Jesus called in a loud voice, "Lazarus, come out!" The dead man came out, his hands and feet wrapped with strips of linen, and a cloth around his face.
>
> Jesus said to them, "Take off the grave clothes and let him go" (John 11:38-44).

We may not be able to raise someone from the dead, but we can point the griever to the person who can. As Paul wrote:

> Brothers, we do not want you to be ignorant about those who fall asleep, or to grieve like the rest of men, who have no hope. We believe that Jesus died and rose again and so we believe that God will bring with Jesus those who have fallen asleep in him (1 Thessalonians 4:13, 14).

I've conducted hundreds of funerals and observed firsthand a significant difference between a Christian and non-Christian funeral. The difference can be defined in one word: hope. We don't sorrow as those who have no hope. There's a huge difference between those who feel they are saying good-bye forever and those who say confidently at the funeral, "See you soon."

It's customary for a minister after preaching a funeral service to stand next to the casket as people pass by and pay their last respects. It can sometimes be gut-wrenching to overhear what close friends and family members whisper to the departed during their moment of intense grief. It's almost sacred ground, and I sometimes feel like an intruder because the comments are so personal and heartfelt. People overcome with emotion will whisper nicknames or childhood expressions in an effort to convey their love one last time.

I watched one woman in her sixties lean over to kiss the body of her mother who was nearly ninety when she passed. Both were committed Christians and loved one another deeply. Fighting back the tears, the daughter kissed her mother on the forehead and whispered, "Nighty-night, Momma. See you in the morning!"

Grief hurts, even for the Christian. But the hope that only Jesus brings comforts us through our tears. Weeping may remain for a night, but the joy of reunion comes in the morning.

Hear the words of Jesus again: "I am the resurrection and the life. He who believes in me will live, even though he dies; and whoever lives and believes in me will never die. Do you believe this?" (John 11:25, 26). If you do, then everything is going to be all right. Jesus promised, "Blessed are those who mourn, for they will be comforted" (Matthew 5:4).

Let's comfort one another with these words.

5

Forgive One Another

King David was at his lowest moment. His own son Absalom was leading a revolution against him. Absalom was a charmer who had convinced many Israelites that David was too old to lead, some fresh blood was needed, and Absalom was just the right man. When Absalom stormed the city with his troops, David and his army fled and left the palace vacant. David decided he'd rather be humiliated in retreat than shed blood in a civil war with his own son.

On the way out of Jerusalem, David must have thought, *It doesn't get any worse than this.* But it did. A bystander by the name of Shimei—a distant relative of David's predecessor King Saul—taunted David as he fled the city. Shimei stood on a hill and threw stones at the king, cursing him and saying, "God is finally punishing you for the way you overthrew King Saul, you bloody traitor!" (2 Samuel 16:5-8).

A heckler interrupted our first service in our new facilities a few years ago. In the middle of my sermon, a homosexual activist stood up and started shouting down at me from the balcony. "That's a lie!" he shouted. "Jesus was humble, and you're not!" (I wondered how he knew me so well.) "Wake up, people!" he continued, "This man is duping you!" Dave Stone and I were team preaching and my part was finished, so I looked at Dave and said, "You're on!" Dave wisely said to the congregation, "You can listen to this person or you can listen to the truth of God's Word. . . ." The congregation interrupted in applause and drowned out the heckler. The policemen serving as our security officers quickly apprehended the man and arrested him for disturbing the peace. I'm glad it wasn't any worse and we still had a good service, but it was hard not to be angry with the guy for selfishly putting a black mark on our first service. The next day papers all over the country read, "Heckler Mars Congregation's First Service in New Building."

It wasn't that difficult, however, for me to get over the heckling I received because it was one of the best days of my ministry and I wasn't going to let him ruin it. I can't imagine how awful it would be if you were heckled on one of the lowest days of your life as David was. One of David's men, Abishai, snarled, "Let me go up and run the impudent coward through with a sword." Everyone assumed the king had a right to execute such a traitor, and they would have all understood if David had said, "Run him through." But King David showed incredible restraint. He told Abishai to let Shimei go. "It may be that the LORD will see my distress and repay me with good for the cursing I am receiving today" David said (2 Samuel 16:12).

If that were the end of the story, we'd say, "What a great man David was. How magnanimous of him to forgive such insubordination." David was a great man, but that's not the end of the story. He didn't get angry and lose his temper, but the memory of that offense festered and stewed in David's heart for years. About ten years later, when David was on his deathbed, here were his final instructions to his son Solomon—the last recorded words of David's life:

> "And remember, you have with you Shimei son of Gera,
> the Benjamite from Bahurim, who called down bitter curs-
> es on me the day I went to Mahanaim. When he came
> down to meet me at the Jordan, I swore to him by the

LORD: 'I will not put you to death by the sword.' But now, do not consider him innocent. You are a man of wisdom; you will know what to do to him. Bring his gray head down to the grave in blood" (1 Kings 2:8, 9).

It's one thing to control your temper when you are first offended. It's quite another to forgive over the long haul and be able to release resentment.

We've all struggled with resentment at times, and some have had to struggle more than others have. If you have been abandoned by your spouse, abused by a parent, victimized by a criminal, hurt by gossip, ripped off by a con man, neglected by your children, overlooked by a coach, put down by a superior, or cheated by relatives, you know what it is like to struggle to forgive. Jesus said we are to forgive seventy times seven (Matthew 18:22, *KJV*). If you've ever been hurt deeply, you know that you may have to forgive someone 490 times for the same offense because you remember it every day.

In his book *Edinburgh Picturesque Notes*, Robert Louis Stevenson told of two spinster ladies who lived together peacefully for years until they had a falling out. They were so bitter toward one another that one of them took a piece of chalk and divided the rooms of the house in half. A chalk line was drawn down the middle of the kitchen, living room, dining room, and each hallway. Each woman refused to acknowledge the presence of the other for the remainder of their lives together. They were separated by chalk lines.[17]

All about us there are chalk lines. We don't see them, but they're there. Certain lines are not to be crossed or there will be civil war. It happens in nearly every area of life—school, business, family, church, sports. But Christians are supposed to be different. We're called to forgive. Jesus taught us to pray, "Forgive us our debts, as we also have forgiven our debtors" (Matthew 6:12). When someone steps over your chalk line, Jesus wants you to forgive.

A Definition of Forgiveness

When you forgive someone, that doesn't mean pretending nothing happened or you weren't hurt. It's not saying what happened was OK. Genuine forgiveness can be defined in two parts. First, forgiveness *relinquishes the right to retaliate*. It's admitting, "I've been wronged, you have hurt me, but I give up my right to hurt you back. Though I have that right, and you deserve it, I give up that right and take the pain upon myself."

Then the forgiveness to which Christ calls us has a second part: Whenever possible, a Christian not only refuses to retaliate but *restores the relationship* as well.

When the prodigal son returned to his father and begged forgiveness, the father had a right to hurt his son back. He could have said, "You wasted all my money! You made a fool of me! You hurt your mother and embarrassed your older brother, and now you come back wanting us to care for you? No way! Hit the road!" The father forgave and gave up his right to make the son pay, and then he went a step further. He restored the relationship. He hugged him, welcomed him back into the home, and threw a party for him, saying, "This son of mine was dead and is alive again; he was lost and is found" (Luke 15:24).

Let me add a note of caution: *There is a difference between forgiveness and reinstating trust.* A child molester who becomes a Christian should be forgiven, but we wouldn't put that man in charge of the toddler department at church. A young woman who discovers her fiancé has been unfaithful can forgive him, but she shouldn't marry him. There are times that it would be unwise to restore the relationship to the same status it had before the offense took place, for example, when you have been the victim of abuse or there have been multiple breaches of trust. Such relationships should never be restored fully without the guidance of a Christian counselor and a lot of prayer. In such instances, "restoring the relationship" may mean simply reaching out with a gesture of kindness to the one who has offended you and acknowledging that the relationship is different but that civility and brotherly kindness can exist between the two of you.

The Difficulty of Forgiveness

Learning to forgive may be the most difficult lesson there is in the Christian life. It's challenging for at least three reasons.

It Goes Against Our Carnal Nature

When I am wronged, I instinctively want to retaliate. That's human nature. If you hit me, I want to hit back. If you cut in front of me in a traffic jam, I want to speed around you and cut you off. If you insult me, I want to insult you back.

When our pride is wounded, our sense of justice demands retaliation. We say, "You'll never get by with this. I'll get even with you if it's the last thing I do. I don't get mad, I get even!" Did you ever stop to think how stupid it is to say, "I'll get even with you"? You're saying, "You are a no good louse, you're as low as a snake, and I'm going to get down there with you and be just like you." Somebody said, "Man is a strange creature. He tries to get ahead of his friends and even with his enemies."

It Requires Trust in the Justice of God

When praying for our enemies, which we'll discuss in chapter nine, we need to remember Romans 12:19, which says, "Do not take revenge, my friends, but leave room for God's wrath, for it is written: 'It is mine to avenge; I will repay,' says the Lord." God says, "Look, I'll see to it that people reap what they sow. If you've been wronged, be patient. I'll make the offender pay." But we have a hard time trusting that God's promise is true, or perhaps we just get impatient and want justice right away. Forgiveness requires trust in God that He will bring about justice in the end.

When King Saul was pursuing David, David hid in a cave.

Saul, unaware that David and his men were there, walked up to that very cave and stood in the mouth of the cave to relieve himself. David's men whispered, "This is your chance! God has given this scoundrel into your hand!"

But David responded, "The LORD forbid that I should do such a thing to my master, the LORD's anointed, or lift my hand against him; for he is the anointed of the LORD" (1 Samuel 24:6). Eventually, Saul was mortally wounded in battle and fell upon his own sword. He died a humiliating death and the nation was eager to have David replace him on the throne. David waited for God's justice to prevail and it did. God saw to it that the one who exalted himself was humbled, and the humble man was exalted.

Pastor and author A. W. Tozer said, "The wheels of God's justice grind slowly, but they grind exceedingly fine." When you take matters into your own hand and seek to retaliate on your own, you throw a monkey wrench into the wheels of God's justice. "It is mine to avenge, I will repay," says the Lord. That takes trust and patience.

It Takes Constant Vigilance

Forgiveness is not usually a single event. It is a continual process. We hear the cliché, "forgive and forget," but the real challenge is to forgive even when you can still remember. One husband said, "Every time my wife and I have an argument she gets historical."

"You mean hysterical?" his friend replied.

"No, historical. She remembers everything I've done wrong!"

God has the power to forget. He says when we come to Him, He "will remember [our] sins no more" (Hebrews 8:12). Man cannot just forget. You might be sincere when you say, "I forgive you," but that doesn't mean you are able to forget about it. If you've ever been hurt deeply, you know that forgiveness is a process and not an instant decision.

Picture a wife whose husband has been unfaithful. She's

devastated. She confronts him. He begs her forgiveness and wants to restore a healthy marriage. After prayer and counsel, she decides to forgive him and restore the relationship. Every day for months she will deal with the pain of that memory. Every day she has to choose to forgive rather than bitterly seek revenge. Even years later, the scar is still there. A few years later she may see an old photograph of that period in their lives and remember how awful she felt. All the emotions surface again, and again she has to choose forgiveness. It may get easier with time, but it takes constant vigilance. As I mentioned earlier, when Jesus said we are to forgive "seventy times seven," it may be for the same serious offense.

The Necessity of Forgiveness

Though it may be difficult, it is essential that we learn to release bitterness and forgive one another. The Bible makes it clear that there is a direct correlation between God's judgment of us and our judgment of others.

In Matthew 18, Jesus told a parable to illustrate the importance of forgiving others: "Therefore, the kingdom of heaven is like a king who wanted to settle accounts with his servants. As he began the settlement, a man who owed him ten thousand talents was brought to him" (vv. 23, 24). Some scholars have estimated that ten thousand talents amounted to over a million dollars in today's currency. Talk about tax problems! This ordinary servant owed the king a million dollars! Jesus continued, "Since he was not able to pay, the master ordered that he and his wife and his children and all that he had be sold to repay the debt."

"The servant fell on his knees before him. 'Be patient with me,' he begged, 'and I will pay back everything'" (Matthew 18:25, 26). There is no way this servant could have repaid that huge debt, but isn't that the way we treat our sins before God? "I'll pay up. Just give me another chance. I'll make up for it. I'll never do it again. I'll be sinless the rest of my life."

Jesus said that despite the irrational bargaining of the servant, the king was merciful. "The servant's master took pity on him, canceled the debt and let him go" (Matthew 18:27).

"Just forget about it," the king said. "I'll take the loss." What a great lesson about God's grace, but the story doesn't end there. Jesus continued:

> "But when that servant went out, he found one of his fellow servants who owed him a hundred denarii [about twenty dollars]. He grabbed him and began to choke him. 'Pay back what you owe me!' he demanded.
>
> "His fellow servant fell to his knees and begged him, 'Be patient with me, and I will pay you back.'
>
> "But he refused. Instead, he went off and had the man thrown into prison until he could pay the debt. When the other servants saw what had happened, they were greatly distressed and went and told their master everything that had happened."
>
> "Then the master called the servant in. 'You wicked servant,' he said, 'I canceled all that debt of yours because you begged me to. Shouldn't you have had mercy on your fellow servant just as I had on you?' In anger his master turned him over to the jailers to be tortured, until he should pay back all he owed" (Matthew 18:28-34).

Of course, the man could never pay back what he owed the king, so he spent the rest of his days in prison because of his unforgiving spirit. Jesus concluded the story with this sobering warning: "This is how my heavenly Father will treat each of you unless you forgive your brother from your heart" (Matthew 18:35).

A man once boasted to John Wesley, "I never forgive." Wesley said, "Well, sir, then I hope you never sin." The Bible repeatedly makes it clear that our relationship with God cannot be right until our relationship with man is correct. If you refuse to forgive others, you can't expect the Lord to forgive you. An unforgiving spirit is extremely dangerous. Jesus said, "And when you stand praying, if you hold anything against anyone, forgive him, so that your Father in heaven may forgive you your sins" (Mark 11:25). Jesus taught us to pray, "Father, forgive us as we forgive those who sin against us."

If you have an unforgiving spirit, it blocks the flow of God's blessing in your life. The Bible says, "And do not grieve the Holy Spirit of God, with whom you were sealed for the day of redemption. Get rid of all bitterness, rage and anger, brawling and slander, along with every form of malice. Be kind and compassionate to one another, forgiving each other, just as in Christ God forgave you" (Ephesians 4:30-32).

God wants to allow His Holy Spirit to flow through you so that your gifts can be used to the fullest. But bitterness, resentment, anger, and revenge act like sewage blocking the flow of God's Spirit. Unforgiveness puts up an obstacle to the grace of God operating in you.

I've never known a happy hater. I've never seen an effective resentful Christian. Hatred creates physical and mental illness, and it destroys your personality. Revenge may be sweet for a moment, but when the immediate pleasure is gone, the damage to you and others that is left behind only makes matters worse. On the other hand, nothing will relieve your burdens like releasing your bitterness to God.

Edwin Markham was a great poet and writer, but his greatest poetry came out of a terrible experience late in his life. He had saved his money for retirement, but just as he was getting ready to retire, someone absconded with his funds. Bitter and hurt because a friend took the money, Markham struggled with resentment and hatred. It kidnapped his thoughts, consumed his being, and took over his life. *I'm in my sixties and I'm broke!* he kept thinking. To make a living, he tried to write poetry, but he couldn't write because he was so obsessed with his hatred.

He finally sat down and began doodling on a paper, just drawing circles and repeating to himself, "I must forgive. I must forgive. I can't even write! I hate this man so much it is destroying my life." He poured out his heart to God, asking Him to cleanse his heart and give him the capacity to forgive. And God did. Markham wrote that he felt as if the heavens opened and a flood came and washed his soul. He started to write again. He saw those circles he had doodled and wrote,

> He drew a circle that shut me out—
> Heretic, rebel, a thing to flout,
> But Love and I had the wit to win:
> We drew a circle and took him in![18]

From that beginning, Markham went on to write the greatest poetry of his life. Why? Obstacles had been removed, barriers had been knocked down, and God's Spirit was allowed to flow in his life.

The Motivation for Forgiveness

Our motivation for forgiveness is that God has forgiven us. That's the point of Jesus' parable in Matthew 18. We've been forgiven a huge debt of sin. Our sin against God is exorbitant—worse than a million-dollar debt. There's no way we could ever repay it. But Christ absorbed the debt at Calvary. He wrote across our account, "Paid in full." Forgiven. How could we not forgive those who have sinned against us when we've been forgiven so much?

Have you ever tried to calculate how many times in a day you sin? Think about the Ten Commandments. Then remember that Jesus said if you lust in your heart, it's the same as committing adultery, and if you hate in your heart, it's the same as committing murder. And remember that the Bible says that anyone "who knows the good he ought to do and doesn't do it, sins" (James 4:17). That's sobering! There are sins of *commission* and sins of *omission*. Every time you think, *I ought to invite my neighbor to church*, and you don't do it; every time you think, *I ought to give my wife a break,* and you don't; or *I need to send a note to that missionary;* or any of a hundred other things you know you ought to do and you don't do it, it's a sin.

So how many times in a day do you sin? Ten? Twenty? Probably more times than that. Let's be ultraconservative and pretend for a moment that you have lived a pretty good life and you only sin about three times a day. You're probably thinking, *In my dreams!* Maybe you can relate to the guy who prayed, "Lord, I haven't hurt anyone today. I haven't said anything harsh to my wife, I haven't exaggerated the truth to my boss, I haven't lost my temper at a driver, I haven't even had a lustful thought. But I'm getting ready to get out of bed and I could really use your help. . . ."

If you could be that good and only sin three times a day, how many sins would you commit in a lifetime? That's about a thousand sins a year (1,095 to be exact). Let's say you live to be eighty years old. We'll count seventy years of sins (supposing you reached a certain "age of accountability" at ten). That would be roughly 70,000 sins in a lifetime! Seventy thousand marks against a holy and righteous God, a perfect God who cannot relate to sin, who cannot stand imperfection in His presence. Are you beginning to relate to the man who carried a debt of a million dollars? Can you see how foolish it must sound for us to say, "I'll pay it back. I'll be good from now on"?

And here's another thing to think about: God has a perfect memory. God isn't bound by time. He exists ever in the present. He sees the past, the present, and the future as clearly as if they were all today. We have a memory that fades with time because He's been gracious enough not to burden us with a perfect memory. However, we can relate a little to what it must be like to be God and remember everything perfectly. Think about the worst offense anyone ever committed against you— the thing that hurt you the most. It is probably etched in your mind as if it happened yesterday. Now imagine—all 70,000 of your sins God can remember as if they happened yesterday. He remembers things that happened four years ago, 400 years ago,

4,000 years ago, as if they just happened. He can recall them perfectly. And He remembers every one of your 70,000 sins. When you stand before Him on judgment day, He's going to look at your life, your 70,000 sins (remember, this is a conservative estimate—and there are some really big ones among the 70,000, I'm sure)—and He is going to be disgusted. Your "good deeds" are going to look like filthy rags compared to all those sins (Isaiah 64:6). The Bible says there is a "dividing wall of hostility" between God and us (Ephesians 2:14). God is not happy with you.

Unless. God is not happy with you *unless* God has chosen to forgive your million-dollar debt of sin. He will remember every one of your sins perfectly *unless* you have surrendered to Jesus Christ and trusted in His salvation. Then God says, "As far as the east is from the west, so far have I removed your sin from you" (Psalm 103:12); "Though your sins are as scarlet, they shall be white as snow" (Isaiah 1:18); "I have hurled your sins into the deepest sea" (Micah 7:19); and, "I will *remember them no more*" (Hebrews 8:12). Max Lucado says, "God has a graciously bad memory."

"Amazing grace! How sweet the sound that saved a *wretch* like me." Through Jesus Christ, the dividing wall of hostility is destroyed and we are reconciled to God (Ephesians 2:14). Our debt has been canceled, praise God!

When I consider how much God has forgiven me, how can I refuse to forgive the one who has wronged me? The debt he owes me is a twenty-dollar debt compared to my sins before God.

Someone said, "We are most like beasts when we kill, most like man when we judge, most like God when we forgive"

During World War II, a father and mother stood at the train station weeping as their only son said good-bye and headed off for overseas duty. The father, fighting back tears, mumbled, "If anything happens to that boy, I hope every Jap in the world gets killed."

Several months later, those parents received the dreaded

telegram from the government. Their son had been killed in action in the Pacific Theater. The father was overwhelmed with grief, resentment, and hatred. For months he would pace the floor at night grinding his teeth, so bitter at the Japanese that it nearly consumed him.

Someone once said that harboring bitterness is like holding a hot coal in your hand, looking for the right moment to hurl it at the person you hate. You are the one getting burned. The bitter father finally recognized that as a Christian, he was commanded to forgive, and he needed to for his own sake. He realized that while he couldn't immediately control his emotions, he could control his actions.

So one day while walking in a nearby park, he prayed and wept and begged God to help him forgive those he hated, to give up his right to retaliate, and to do his best to restore a right relationship with his fellow man.

God gave him the victory. Months later, when those godly parents received a sizeable check from their insurance company for the death benefits of their son, a sizable portion of that check was given to their church and earmarked for mission work in Japan.

Forgiveness is difficult, but it's possible even for those who have been deeply hurt. "Do not be overcome by evil," the Bible says, "but overcome evil with good" (Romans 12:21).

Is there someone you need to forgive? If so, I hope you will take steps today toward forgiveness. Under some circumstances, it will take a lot of help. You may need to seek out a Christian counselor. You may need to confront the person who wronged you so that blame is placed where it belongs and then forgiveness can begin. Or maybe you need to seek the forgiveness of someone you have wronged. Pray that God will lead you and give you the strength to release your bitterness. Then begin today to live a life of forgiveness, remembering all that you have been forgiven.

6

Honor One Another

On December 3, 1979, thousands of young people stood outside Riverfront Coliseum in Cincinnati, Ohio, anxiously waiting for the gates to open for the Who rock concert that evening. The seating was all general admission, no reserved seats. People had been waiting for hours so they could be the first in the stadium and rush to the front for the best seats. The crowd was growing more restless with each passing minute. When the gates were finally opened, there was a mad scramble to get the best seats. The frantic pushing and shoving at the gate caused tragic results. The massive crowd crushed several who fell beneath them as those who were being pushed from behind were left with little choice but to continue forward. When the incredible sequence of events was over, eleven people had been trampled to death.

That incident is a grim reminder of the selfish ambition of man. The intense concern for the chief seats resulted in the loss of lives and considerable grief. That kind of self-interest goes on all the time in the everyday world, though the wounds are not always as immediately visible. People are determined to get ahead no matter whom they have to step on or injure to get there.

Jesus sought to counter that spirit of self-promotion. He

challenged us to honor one another above ourselves. He got a
great opportunity to teach this lesson when He visited the
home of a prominent Pharisee as recorded in Luke 14. The
Pharisees were a proud, self-righteous group. Outwardly, they
were very religious—they fasted twice a week, tithed their
income, prayed three times a day, and memorized large
amounts of Scripture, but it was all for show. Inwardly, many
of them were egotistical and very conscious of their social status. Their religiosity was performed to enhance their image.

In this particular instance, in fact, they had invited Jesus to a
banquet under false pretenses. Their jealousy of Jesus' popularity had gotten the best of them, and they hoped to trick Him
into making a blunder. Luke wrote, "One Sabbath, when Jesus
went to eat in the house of a prominent Pharisee, he was being
carefully watched" (14:1).

Before the meal began, a man suffering from dropsy, a kind
of nervous disorder, came into the room. Most likely the afflict-
ed man was a plant. There he was, so conveniently in front of
Jesus, needing to be healed on the Sabbath. The Pharisees were
not above exploiting a handicapped person if it meant advanc-
ing their cause and enhancing their own image. They knew
Jesus' reputation for healing, and they knew that if He healed
on the Sabbath, they could charge Him for violating their strict
laws, which forbade anyone to perform his trade, like practicing medicine, on the Sabbath.

Jesus would not be cornered. He dealt with the situation
directly, asking the Pharisees and experts in the law, "Is it law-
ful to heal on the Sabbath or not?" (Luke 14:3). They cowardly
remained silent, so Jesus healed the man and sent him on his
way. Then He turned to his critics and said, "If one of you has a
son or an ox that falls into a well on the Sabbath day, will you
not immediately pull him out?" (Luke 14:5). They had no
response. In one simple illustration Jesus had revealed their
inconsistency and arrogance.

Apparently that premeal incident wasn't enough to humble
the proud Pharisees. When it was dinnertime, Jesus noticed

them scrambling for the chief seats at the table. The tables at such a banquet were usually U-shaped, and the honored guest would sit at the head in the middle of the "U." The places to his immediate right and left were reserved for the next most honored and then the others were seated around the table in descending order of importance. Jesus watched them slyly maneuver themselves for the chief seats. Their arrogance prompted Him to tell a parable.

"A man came to a banquet," Jesus said, "and plopped himself down in the chief seat. Later, he had to be asked to move down."

That's humiliating, to say the least. It's degrading when you discover that your opinion of yourself is so much higher than others' opinion of you. Years ago, a friend and I were invited to hear the governor of Kentucky speak at a luncheon in downtown Louisville. When we arrived, many had already sat down around the banquet tables and there were not many seats left. We noticed that a round table next to the platform was still vacant, so we sat down and congratulated ourselves for getting such good seats. A few minutes later, an usher tapped us on the shoulder and said, "I'm sorry. This table is reserved for the chief of police and his party." It was so humiliating to have to get up and walk through the crowd and stand in the back!

Jesus continued, "When you're invited to a banquet, take the lowest place. Maybe then the host will invite you to move up to a better seat, and you will be honored in front of the other guests."

This is not just a parable about proper etiquette and politeness, but also a lesson about the spirit of honor that Christians should have toward one another—a lesson that's badly needed in an era of self-service and self-promotion.

The World Instinctively Pushes for Places of Prominence

Humans have always been self-centered, but selfishness and pride seem to be more dominant in our American culture today.

Maybe it's because we have smaller families and it's easier to be self-centered. Years ago when families had six, seven, eight, or even more children, everyone learned to sacrifice out of necessity. Now, with smaller families of only two or three children, it's easy to grow up thinking the world revolves around you.

Or maybe our self-centeredness is more prominent because we live in such affluence. In the past, people couldn't afford many of the things they wanted and so they became accustomed to self-denial. But today, if you really want something, you can often get it—and get it right away—with no money down! The most entertaining toys, music, and video games are available to children relatively inexpensively, and we get used to having just about anything we want from the time we are young.

Maybe we're more self-centered because of constant exposure to skilled advertising. The media stimulates ego-centered thinking, promising happiness, friendship, and fulfillment if you indulge yourself. Use a certain skin lotion and you will be the object of adoration. Buy the right car and the prettiest girls will ride with you. Drink the right soft drink and you'll never go thirsty again. In a world where selfishness is encouraged for the sake of sales, it's difficult to get people to recognize how desperately empty the life of the selfish person really is.

The evidence of self-promotion is all around us. In business, the mahogany desk outranks the walnut desk, which outranks the oak, and there can be bitter competition for the positions of prominence. In school there are classes and seminars on self-assertion. There aren't many classes on humility and self-sacrifice. The courts are full of frivolous lawsuits because people are intent on demanding their rights. Our whole society is consumed with self—my image, my status, my attention, my happiness, and my rights.

Self-promotion can infiltrate the church, too, if we're not careful. I've seen people refuse to be supportive of the leadership because their friend wasn't considered for chairman of the board. People get their feelings hurt if they don't get a part in the Easter pageant or they aren't invited to sing a solo during the service. I was once preparing to speak at a revival meeting when, before the service began, someone with a guitar walked up to the worship leader and asked if he could sing a song in the service. When he was told no, he stomped off in a huff.

William Barclay once said, "More than half of the trouble that arises in church concerns rights, places, privileges and prestige. Someone has not been given his or her place, someone hasn't been thanked, someone has been neglected, someone has been given a more prominent place on the platform than someone else and there's trouble."

It's not just in church that Christians are tempted to battle selfishness. How many good marriages have dissolved because of a drive for prominence? How much heartache have young people caused their parents because of their unwillingness to give up their pride? How many times have we heaped financial burdens on ourselves because we purchased things primarily for appearance? How many poor career choices have we made because we were too concerned about our image?

God Consistently Exalts the Humble

Jesus promised that the person who is humble enough to honor others above himself will ultimately be exalted. "For everyone who exalts himself will be humbled, and he who humbles himself will be exalted," he said (Luke 14:11).

Sometimes that exaltation doesn't take place until Heaven where "the last will be first, and the first will be last" (Matthew

20:16). But even in this world, it is usually true that the humble person is ultimately exalted and used by God. In his book *Good to Great*, an outstanding secular book on leadership, Jim Collins documented the qualities of what he calls a "Level Five Leader." He spent years analyzing what made some companies continue to prosper for decades. One of the most notable characteristics among companies that moved "from good to great" and sustained it for many years was a CEO who exhibited an attitude of unselfishness and humility. Collins said Level Five leaders build enduring greatness through a paradoxical blend of personal humility and professional will. "We found leaders of this type at the helm of every good to great company," he wrote.[19]

Collins added:

> Good-to-great leaders didn't talk much about themselves . . . but would deflect discussion about their own contributions. When pressed to talk about themselves, they said things like, "I hope I'm not sounding like a big shot. . . ." Or, "There are plenty of people in this company who could do my job better than I do." It wasn't just a false modesty. Those who worked with or wrote about good-to-great leaders continually used words like quiet, humble, modest, reserved, shy, gracious, mild-mannered, self-effacing, understated, did not believe his own press clippings; and so forth. . . . The good-to-great leaders never wanted to become larger-than-life heroes. They never aspired to be put on a pedestal or become unreachable icons. They were seemingly ordinary people quietly producing extraordinary results.[20]

Collins noted that good-to-great leaders were more like Abraham Lincoln and less like General George Patton. Even the secular world acknowledges that Jesus' promise rings true—the proud are humbled and the humble are exalted.

If God Exalts You, Accept It!

By the way, if God or God's people grant you a position of honor, be willing to accept it. We shouldn't carry false humility around with us, saying, "Oh, I could never sit at the head table." I know people who have a martyr complex and are always insisting on sitting in the back seat of the car or being last in line. It's not humility; it's self-consciousness or self-righteousness, and it is often a disguised attempt to attract attention.

I know of a couple who attended a wedding for a family member and the usher mistakenly sat them in the back instead of with the rest of the bride's family. When the mistake was discovered, the usher approached them, apologized, and offered to escort them to the front. But the couple stubbornly refused. "Oh, no," they said in mock humility, "this seat is fine." And they pouted all the more, drawing greater attention to themselves than if they had moved up to the more prominent seats.

Do not manipulate the situation to get the better seat, as Jesus said, and do not promote yourself. If the position is earned or offered, accept it. Somebody has to sit up front. Jesus did when He was invited to do so. Somebody has to lead. If God has gifted you or appointed you, accept the role willingly. Don't put forth a false humility and make people beg or bribe you to take the role. Whatever you do, do it with a congenial spirit and dependence on God.

The Christian Is to Obediently Defer to Others

Jesus' lesson in Luke 14 is that we are to honor one another above ourselves. "When someone invites you to a wedding feast, do not take the place of honor" (v. 8). To defer to others isn't easy. It's absolutely contrary to this age. People will consider you weird, and you may not get ahead as quickly as others. And it's contrary to your carnal nature. Your heart tells you that if you don't blow your own horn, nobody else will. But to honor others above yourself is consistent with the character of Christ and with the commands of Scripture, and God promises to reward you in the end if you honor others above yourself.

Commanded in Scripture

"Honor one another above yourselves," the Bible commands (Romans 12:10). "Do nothing out of selfish ambition or vain conceit, but in humility consider others better than yourselves. Each of you should look not only to your own interests, but also to the interests of others" (Philippians 2:3, 4).

The church in Philippi sent Epaphroditus to minister to Paul while he was imprisoned in Rome. Somewhere along the line, Epaphroditus contracted an illness that nearly took his life. He was probably a little embarrassed that he wasn't more help to Paul. When Paul sent him back to the Philippians, he encouraged them to give him a hero's welcome. He wrote:

> I think it is necessary to send back to you Epaphroditus, my brother, fellow worker and fellow soldier, who is also your messenger, whom you sent to take care of my needs. For he longs for all of you and is distressed because you heard he was ill. Indeed he was ill, and almost died. But God had mercy on him. . . . Welcome him in the Lord with great joy, and *honor men like him*, because he almost died for the work of Christ, risking his life to make up for the help you could not give me (Philippians 2:25-30, emphasis mine).

Instead of pointing out the failures of someone like Epaphroditus in an effort to make ourselves look better, we are commanded to honor a person for his dedication and be willing to acknowledge the heroic or sacrificial efforts of someone else. "Clothe yourselves with humility toward one another," the Bible says, "because 'God opposes the proud but gives grace to the humble' " (1 Peter 5:5).

Exemplified by Christ

On the last night of Jesus' life, while Jesus agonized over the suffering He knew He was about to endure, a quarrel arose among His disciples as to which of them was the greatest. We don't know how the argument began, but since Jesus had gathered the group to eat the Passover meal together (the most important observance of the year for the Jews), it's likely that the strife arose over the seating arrangements at the meal.

What a tragedy that in His last hours, Jesus had to witness His own disciples, into whom He had poured His life for the last three years, scrambling like the Pharisees for seats of distinction.

Jesus asked them, "Who is greater, the one who is at the table or the one who serves?" (Luke 22:27). Then He got up, took off His outer garment, wrapped himself with a towel as a servant would do, and washed the feet of the disciples. They sat dumbfounded, utterly disgraced. It was hardly necessary for Jesus to remind them to do as He had done. The Son of God was washing their feet. That was a lesson they wouldn't forget.

Needed in the Church

It's a lesson we need to remember, too. You might say, "But if I humble myself and exalt others, I'll be a doormat. People will run over top of me." Probably not. In the long run, God will exalt you and people will respect you because of your servant's heart. Even if they do take advantage of you, nobody was more victimized than Jesus Christ, and God has given us His Son as an example for us to follow.

You might also say, "If I serve others, I'll be miserable." That, too, is false. Selfish people are miserable. Humble people who willingly serve others are the happiest people in the world. Jesus said, "Whoever wants to save his life will lose it, but whoever loses his life for me will find it" (Matthew 16:25).

I can think of several practical ways we can seek to honor others above ourselves.

Cut out all sarcasm and criticism from your vocabulary.
The Bible says, "Reckless words pierce like a sword, but the tongue of the wise brings healing" (Proverbs 12:18). You might think your sarcastic comments are funny, and they might elicit nervous laughter from others, but they are piercing someone's heart. You might think the person you're attacking is arrogant and deserving, but you are not the judge. And, usually, your biting tongue is an indication of your own insecurities and desire to measure up by cutting another person down.

Rick Stedman, minister of the Adventure Christian Church in Roseville, California, has a "no sarcasm" rule for his church staff. He says that what makes people laugh at sarcasm is that it always has a nugget of truth in it. That little bit of truth is what hurts people. So "no sarcasm" is the rule. "Don't exploit others' weaknesses or embarrass someone to get a cheap laugh," Stedman suggests. "If you can't be kind, don't say anything at all."

Anyone can cut others down. Only a wise, mature person knows how to reign in his tongue and use it to bring healing. James wrote:

> All kinds of animals, birds, reptiles and creatures of the sea are being tamed and have been tamed by man, but no man can tame the tongue. It is a restless evil, full of deadly poison.
>
> With the tongue we praise our Lord and Father, and with it we curse men, who have been made in God's likeness. Out of the same mouth come praise and cursing. My brothers, this should not be. Can both fresh water and salt water flow from the same spring? My brothers, can a fig tree bear olives, or a grapevine bear figs? Neither can a salt spring produce fresh water (3:7-12).

Do something menial in service to others. I preached at a large church in Indianapolis recently. Afterward, an elderly woman approached me and asked if I knew Marc and Yumiko Leis. I said, "Yes, they are members of our church and we've been supporting their work in Japan for years." She was delighted. She said, "Our Sunday school class has been supporting them too! In fact, we've been collecting toys for them for several weeks. I've got three bags of toys to send to them. I know they're in Louisville right now. Would you be willing to take those bags of toys back to them in Louisville if I brought them into the building?"

That may seem like a small request, but I knew it would mean at least another five minutes of my time as I waited for her to leave and come back and then have further dialogue with her. Plus it would mean loading the toys into my car on a cold day. Then I would have to load my luggage into the backseat because there would be no more room in the trunk. Then, when I got to Louisville, I would have to figure out what to do with all those toys! At the very least, I would have to lug them up to the Missions Department at Southeast, a long haul from where I usually park my car.

I was tempted to say, "I'm not the UPS man! I'm the preacher of a very large church!" But I know the many examples of Jesus serving others, so I loaded my trunk with toys and lugged them up to the Missions Department the next day. I probably won't get much of a reward in Heaven for that act of service because my heart wasn't much into it, but at least I didn't set a bad example!

All of us want the prominent service roles; we want to teach the class, sing the solo, coach the team, or pray at the table. For many of us, as we grow older we gain more and more prestige and we have to do menial tasks less often. Go out of your way to do something in service to someone who can't reward you. Cut your neighbor's grass, serve in the nursery, volunteer to clean the bathrooms at church, or do a chore for a family member. Determine that you are regularly going to do those things that should be "beneath" you to remind you that you aren't that great and that other people are worthy of service and honor. And occasionally do it anonymously. The God who sees in secret will reward you!

Look for an opportunity to encourage someone. Paul commanded, "Encourage one another and build each other up, just as in fact you are doing" (1 Thessalonians 5:11). Everyone needs to be encouraged. Your minister, your teacher, the young person going off to college, your spouse, your neighbor's son in the military, your friend who just got promoted, your relative who just lost his job—all of them need and want to be lifted up. Find a practical way to encourage someone every day. Write a note, say thank you, pat him on the back and say "good job!"

Last summer I visited the church of a young preacher who grew up in our congregation. On Monday morning, I wrote him a brief note complimenting the sermon and telling him how proud I was of his ministry. His father recently said to me, "Barry's congregation recently moved into their new building. Do you remember that letter you wrote Barry last year? He had it framed and it's sitting beside his desk in his new office." You never know how much just a little encouragement can mean to someone. I wish I had taken the time to do that kind of thing more often in my years of ministry.

Give honor to whom honor is due. "Honor men like him," Paul wrote of Epaphroditus, "because he almost died for the work of Christ" (Philippians 2:29, 30). Occasionally, it's appropriate to give special honor to those who deserve recognition for their service to Christ. Our children need real heroes and our church members need inspiration. When a missionary comes home from the field, when a longtime minister retires, when a member of the church serves in a special way, it's appropriate that we give that person special honor.

Nobody I know does this better than Wayne Smith, the beloved retired minister of Southland Christian Church in Lexington, Kentucky. Wayne is a great gift-giver and is wonderful at giving honor to whom honor is due. There must be hundreds of ministers, missionaries, and church members who have received plaques and gifts from Wayne Smith at special times in their lives. Wayne's church has for many years been the second-largest church in Kentucky, behind Southeast. You would think that the minister of the second-largest church would jealously compete with the largest congregation and sneer and scoff at the successes of the other, but Wayne has been my biggest supporter. In my office are several plaques I received from Wayne when Southeast reached a milestone. A building campaign that reached its goal, a significant anniversary or record attendance day is bound to bring a gift of recognition from Wayne Smith. The one the world would vote least likely to rejoice with me has been the most likely to do so. And you know what? We respect him and honor him so much more because he puts others ahead of himself.

7

Bear One Another's Burdens

My daughter-in-law Kellie wanted to help bear the burden for her brother Brian Freeman, who was enduring thirteen weeks of marine boot camp in Paris Island, South Carolina. Kellie knew that Brian's training period would be a physically and spiritually trying time, so she shared Brian's address with her Adult Bible Fellowship class and asked them to send encouraging letters to her brother. One of the members of the class decided to go the extra mile and sent a Kentucky Derby Pie to Brian. What a thoughtful gesture, you might think.

Marine recruits, however, aren't allowed to receive packages from home. Desserts are especially forbidden because the drill instructors are trying to get the young recruits in top physical condition. It is the job of the recruit to inform his friends and family members not to send such items. If his family members don't comply, the recipient is publicly humiliated. Brian had told Kellie, "Don't even send a colored envelope or anything that attracts attention." The drill instructors looked for any opportunity to embarrass a recruit. The message hadn't gotten through to one member of the ABF class, and Brian paid for it dearly!

When the package arrived, the drill instructor said, "Well, well, what do we have here? Freeman! You've got a package!

From Louisville, Kentucky." The instructor opened it. "Lookie here! It's a Derby Pie! It's been a long time since any of you had chocolate. Wouldn't that be yummy? Maybe we could all get a chocolate pie. Wouldn't that be wonderful? Look! It has baking instructions. It says right here, bake at 300 degrees." His voice dripped with sarcasm as he asked, "Does anyone here have an oven?"

Brian wound up doing a brutal series of exercises for a prolonged period in "the pit," a sand pit where he had to battle sand fleas as well as the South Carolina summer sun. He called his mother and said, "Tell Kellie to ask her class not to care anymore!"

There are a lot of places in the world that aren't noted for their kindness and compassion—the military, business world, political arena, and sports world are places where being compassionate is looked down upon. Christians have an opportunity to present a stark contrast to the world by caring for one another, especially in times of need. The Bible commands us to "bear . . . one another's burdens" (Galatians 6:2, *KJV*).

Jesus Set the Example

There are dozens of examples of Jesus reaching out to someone in need. In this chapter, let's look closely at just one—the healing of blind Bartimaeus. Luke tells us, "As Jesus approached Jericho, a blind man was sitting by the roadside begging" (18:35). Mark's Gospel says the man's name was Bartimaeus (10:46), and Matthew tells us that Bartimaeus had a blind friend with him (20:30).[21]

"Jesus, Son of David, have mercy on me!" Bartimaeus shouted (Luke 18:38).

Turley Richards, a member of our congregation, lost his eyesight when he was a young man. He's an amazing person. Years ago, before he became a Christian, he had three top *Billboard* hits that sold almost a million and a half copies. Turley now runs his own music business from his home, mostly by phone. He's not only talented, but he has a great sense of humor, too. He says that sometimes people with whom he's conversed many times on the phone suddenly discover that he's blind. They'll say, "Funny, you don't sound blind." He'll say, "Funny, you don't sound stupid either!" I once asked our men's Bible study for volunteers to help park cars, and Turley raised his hand! When I pointed him out, he just laughed and so did everyone else. He's a joy to be around and an inspiration to all who know him.

Though many blind people like Turley can do amazing things and are an inspiration to us, blindness is still a tragic disability. I asked Turley what he missed most about not being able to see. He said, "I miss not being able to shoot a basketball or play pool, but mostly I miss never being able to see my kids. If God gave me two minutes of sight, I'd give one minute to each child."

It would be tough not to be able to see your children's faces or witness their activities. It would be difficult to not see the beauty of the changing leaves, to never see a sunset or snow-capped mountain, and to never watch a ball game, movie, or parade. It was even more tragic in the first century when there were no phones, no trained dogs, no books on tape, no Braille, no computers that talked back, and no sidewalks to serve as guided paths to a destination. People were less sympathetic and there was no government assistance, so most blind people were destined to do what Bartimaeus did—he sat daily by the road and begged for a handout.

Jesus asked Bartimaeus, "What do you want me to do for you?"

"Lord, I want to see," he replied (Luke 18:41).

Author Ken Gire observed that Jesus knew what the man meant:

> I want out of the dungeon, out of the darkness. I want out
> of the shackles of these blind eyes. . . . I want to get off of

the roadside. I want to walk the streets of Jericho without
running into its walls. I want to look in the shops. I want to
find my way to the Synagogue. . . . I want to use my hands
for something besides feeling my way in the dark. . . . I
want to fix my own meals. I want to read. . . . I want to
wave at someone across the way. I want to smile at children
and pat their heads and wish them well. . . . I want to see.[22]

Jesus had mercy on the man and said to him, "Receive your
sight; your faith has healed you." Luke records what happened
next: "Immediately he received his sight and followed Jesus,
praising God. When all the people saw it, they also praised
God" (18:42, 43).

In the twinkling of an eye, Bartimaeus went from darkness to
light. He was once blind, but now he could see. Gire concluded:

Sunshine floods his eyes. He sees the azure sky . . . the
armada of clouds in full sail . . . the pair of turtledoves
winging their way just above the rooftops. He sees the
buildings . . . the amazed faces of the crowd. . . . And then
he turns and sees Jesus. He sees the tenderness. He sees
the love. He sees the eyes of a king.[23]

We may not be able to take away someone's burden like
Jesus could, but we should want to! If you love someone, you
wish you were able to take his burden away, and you want to
do what you can to help him bear the load he is under. Jesus
had mercy on the man. He would have had no less mercy had
He not been able to heal Bartimaeus. He would have responded differently, but He would have responded nonetheless.

Following the Example of Christ

The Bible instructs us to follow Christ's example of burden
bearing. "Carry each other's burdens," Paul wrote, "and in this
way you will fulfill the law of Christ" (Galatians 6:2).

Bearing Financial Burdens

The Bible commands, "Speak up for those who cannot speak for themselves, for the rights of all who are destitute. Speak up and judge fairly; defend the rights of the poor and needy" (Proverbs 31:8, 9). In Acts, we learn that the early church provided for the poor among them:

> All the believers were one in heart and mind. No one claimed that any of his possessions was his own, but they shared everything they had. . . . There were no needy persons among them. For from time to time those who owned lands or houses sold them, brought the money from the sales and put it at the apostles' feet, and it was distributed to anyone as he had need (4:32-35).

The early church was supported by the sacrificial gifts of individual Christians. They didn't develop a fund-raising scheme to get people in the world to pay their bills. They didn't have a raffle or carnival, or hold a bazaar at the temple. They gave of their own wealth to respond to the needs of other Christians.

As we consider our obligation to help bear the financial burden of those among us, let's make some important observations about the way the early church bore the burdens of the poor.

Notice first that their gifts were voluntary sacrifices, not a mandatory assessment placed upon each member. This was not a socialistic system where everyone was prohibited from owning anything. Because they all sensed the extreme importance of financing the first church and missionary efforts, nearly all of the wealthy people voluntarily gave everything they had for the cause.

Notice also that their giving was organized, not haphazard. The church members didn't just indiscriminately give money to the poor. They brought the money to the apostles, who used discernment in distributing the funds. Some was used for the advancement of the gospel and some for bearing the burdens of the poor. Sometimes it's good for an individual to see a need and respond on his own, but we are wise to trust the church to meet ongoing benevolent needs. Then we ensure that our own motives are pure, and there is a greater chance that deserving people will receive the help they need. Often the most deserving people are too humble to ask for help, and the least deserving are great at marketing their "plight" and milking the system. If capable leadership is running your church, the leadership should be trusted to take care of the poor. If capable leadership is not running it, go somewhere else!

Notice thirdly that the money was given to those who had need, not just to those who had less. In a socialistic system, everybody gets an equal distribution of the wealth (except for those in charge, who tend to be the only wealthy members of a socialistic culture). In the early church, the money was distributed to people "as they had need."

Zacchaeus was a wealthy man. He met Jesus and said, "Lord! Here and now I give half of my possessions to the poor" (Luke 19:8). Jesus didn't say, "Zacchaeus, that's not enough. You should give it all." He commended Zacchaeus and said, "Today salvation has come to this house" (Luke 19:9).

The Bible doesn't teach equal distribution of wealth, but generosity to the needy. "If anyone has material possessions and sees his brother in need but has no pity on him, how can the love of God be in him?" John asked (1 John 3:17). Notice he didn't say, "If you see someone with an older car than yours, a smaller house or less meat . . ." but, "if you see your brother in need."

Acts 6 gives another example of the early church ministering to financial needs. "In those days when the number of disciples was increasing, the Grecian Jews among them complained against the Hebraic Jews because their widows were being overlooked in the daily distribution of food" (v. 1). One of our church's long-time elders, John Foster, spent many years as the chairman of the benevolence committee. He talked about the challenges facing a congregation in today's American society.

He said, "The Bible tells us in James that religion that is pure and undefiled is to care for the widows and orphans. The modern-day analogy to that are the divorced women with children. Regardless of the circumstances that got them into their situation, they need help. If the church doesn't help them, we almost force them to remarry in order to survive. That means sometimes we have to commit ourselves to long-term assistance. It's easy to care briefly, but more difficult to care and be sensitive repeatedly."

Peter Ustinov said, "Charity is more common than compassion. Charity is tax-deductible. Compassion is time consuming." The Bible commands, "Give proper recognition to those widows who are really in need" (1 Timothy 5:3).

The early church apparently had a welfare program to care for its widows. People gave money so that the church could provide a food closet and other necessities. Some of the widows began complaining that they weren't getting their fair share, and the apostles knew something had to be done to ensure the proper administration of the benevolence program. "So the Twelve gathered all the disciples together and said, 'It would not be right for us to neglect the ministry of the word of God in order to wait on tables'" (Acts 6:2). The apostles recognized their responsibility to help bear the burdens of those in need, but they wanted to remain true to their primary calling—teaching people God's Word. They came up with a plan: "Brothers, choose seven men from among you who are known to be full of the Spirit and wisdom. We will turn this responsibility over to them and will give our attention to prayer and the ministry of the word" (Acts 6:3, 4). That idea pleased the whole group. They selected seven capable men and delegated the responsibility to them. And Luke mentions that the Word of God continued to spread as a result. There may be no better testimony to the world than tangible expressions of compassion by the church.

A Jewish man with whom I occasionally play golf once remarked to me, "I don't agree with what your church teaches,

but I sure do appreciate the way you help needy people."
Those outside our church walls may not listen to our message
at first, but deeds of compassion for the needy will soften their
hearts and make them more receptive to the gospel.

But there are so many needs! How do you know who is
deserving of help? The Bible gives us a couple of qualifiers:

**First, we are to help those who are willing to work, not the
lazy.** "For even when we were with you," Paul wrote, "we gave
you this rule: 'If a man will not work, he shall not eat'" (2
Thessalonians 3:10). If you keep giving food to a man who is
capable of earning it and has the opportunity to do so, you
aren't helping him. You're robbing him of the dignity of work
and encouraging his laziness. When you see a person on the
side of the road with a sign that says, "Will work for food,"
offer to give him a job doing chores at your church or place of
business for a fair wage. If he refuses, he doesn't want to eat
badly enough. It's important that Christians wisely discern the
difference between a person with legitimate financial burdens
and one who is disguising his own laziness. Giving a handout
to an undeserving person is poor stewardship and can do more
harm than good.

But remember, when you're trying to determine whether
someone's need is legitimate or not, it is impossible to discern
rightly every time. Err on the side of grace. I'd rather be taken
for granted a couple of times than miss the opportunity to
help someone who has a legitimate need. I love the story
about professional golfer Roberto de Vicenzo who was
approached after a big victory by a woman wanting a handout. She wept that her daughter was dying of cancer but might
survive if she had a thousand dollars for an experimental
medication. After the golfer wrote out a check and she had
gone her way, someone told him the lady's daughter didn't
really have cancer. The golfer said, "She doesn't? That's the
best news I've heard all day!" Our attitude toward those with
financial burdens should be one of compassion and grace, not
skepticism and bitterness.

Secondly, we are to help other believers first. "Therefore, as we have opportunity, let us do good to all people, especially to those who belong to the family of believers" (Galatians 6:10). We should meet as many legitimate needs as possible, but our first responsibility is to help bear the burdens of those in our own ranks.

Bearing Physical Burdens

The early church also ministered to people with physical burdens. The book of Acts records:

> More and more men and women believed in the Lord and were added to their number. As a result, people brought the sick into the streets and laid them on beds and mats so that at least Peter's shadow might fall on some of them as he passed by. Crowds gathered also from the towns around Jerusalem, bringing their sick and those tormented by evil spirits, and all of them were healed (5:14-16).

Maybe we can't offer immediate healing like Peter did, but we can help people bear their physical burdens by easing their suffering and praying for them. The Bible commands, "Is any one of you sick? He should call the elders of the church to pray over him and anoint him with oil in the name of the Lord. And the prayer offered in faith will make the sick person well; the Lord will raise him up" (James 5:14, 15).

Many of our hospitals exist today because churches cared enough about bringing healing and providing compassion that they began a place to care for the sick. You can walk the halls of any hospital in America and run into clergy, ministers, and laypeople who are there in the name of Christ to comfort and pray for the sick.

Ministries like Prison Fellowship exist not only to bring Christ to those in prison but also to be advocates for fairness, cleanliness, decency, and real reform programs in our prisons. They've also done outstanding work in reaching out to the families of those in prison through programs like Project Angel Tree.

I'm proud of places like Christian Church Foundation for the Handicapped that are ministering to people with mental and physical handicaps.

And crisis pregnancy centers have cropped up in every major city in America, ministering to women in need and giving them alternatives to abortion. The head of one of our crisis pregnancy centers in Louisville told me about a woman who had scheduled to have an abortion the following week but came into the center for help. She thought she had no options. Her boyfriend had just broken up with her and she was on drugs. A loving volunteer helped provide a free ultrasound, which revealed to the young woman that a fully formed baby was already growing inside of her. The girl decided that day not to kill the infant forming inside her. During her pregnancy, a lasting relationship developed between the new mother and the volunteer from the pregnancy center. They met for lunch from time to time, celebrated birthdays, and attended birthing classes together. The volunteer was even the young lady's labor coach. The young mother attended college during her pregnancy and stopped her drug use and cigarette smoking. Today she is the mother of a beautiful baby girl and has given her life to Christ.

We could certainly do better in many of these areas, and we need to remember that each of us will stand before God and give account for our personal efforts to bear one another's burdens, but I'm thankful that so many opportunities exist to do so in our churches today. Jesus said that on judgment day He would say to those on His right hand:

> Come, you who are blessed by my Father; take your inheritance, the kingdom prepared for you since the creation of the world. For I was hungry and you gave me something to eat, I was thirsty and you gave me something to drink, I was a stranger and you invited me in, I needed clothes and you clothed me, I was sick and you looked after me, I was in prison and you came to visit me (Matthew 25:34-36).

Jesus said that the righteous will ask, "Lord, when did we see you in need of these things and provide them?" And He will answer, "I tell you the truth, whatever you did for one of the least of these brothers of mine, you did for me" (Matthew 25:40).

Bearing Emotional and Spiritual Burdens

Jesus said, "I was a stranger—I was lonely—and you took me in. I was in prison—I felt rejected—and you came and visited me." The apostle Paul had his emotional needs met while he was encountering various trials because his brothers and sisters in Christ comforted and encouraged him. He later wrote:

> [God] comforts us in all our troubles, so that we can comfort those in any trouble with the comfort we ourselves have received from God. For just as the sufferings of Christ flow over into our lives, so also through Christ our comfort overflows. If we are distressed, it is for your comfort and salvation (2 Corinthians 1:4-6).

The church is to be a place where people bear one another's burdens by comforting each other in times of emotional pain. Churches are doing better today at providing counseling for those who have deep emotional scars and organizing support groups for those who have been through addictions, divorce, cancer, the death of a child, or other tragedies. We could do better, but we're learning how to minister to the emotional needs of people.

The darker our world becomes, the more necessary these kinds of ministries will be. One minister, commenting about the number of people left hurting in our world because of sin, said, "I feel like I'm walking over a battlefield after the battle, trying to care for the wounded."

Ministering to the needy is not just the task of the institutional church, but of the individual Christian as well. Sometimes people excuse their unwillingness to bear the burdens of others by blaming the church. People will ask, "Why doesn't the church do something about the hungry?" Or "Why don't the leaders organize an effective ministry to the children of single parents?"

One member of our church, Kathy Drane, felt compassion for an orphan she met while she was on a short-term mission trip to Ukraine. Kathy was over forty years old and her only child was nearly a teenager. She thought she was through having babies long ago, but her heart went out to the little girl and she decided to adopt her. Kathy's example motivated many others to consider adopting one of the many neglected orphans in countries like Ukraine. Kathy helped so many other families adopt children that she began her own adoption agency. As a result of her help, over eighty Ukranian orphans have been adopted by Christian families in America. She's now working to establish an organization called Hopeful, which is dedicated to helping older children who rarely get adopted and to improving the facilities and care of those left behind in Ukraine.

Church leaders do need to coordinate programs to minister to the needy, but much of what the church does is through individuals like Kathy Drane. Sometimes we need to be willing to get our own hands dirty and respond to the need ourselves. When we do, through the church or through our own efforts, we are helping to "bear one another's burdens."

8

Encourage One Another

Jesus was an encourager. Throughout the Gospels, we see Him lifting people up. He would grab the lame man by the hand, touch the leper, weep with the grieving sisters, or say the ultimate encouragement to the sinner, "Your sins are forgiven." Jesus knew that even more than good health, a strong spirit sustains us in difficult times.

The Bible says, "And let us consider how we may spur one another on toward love and good deeds. Let us not give up meeting together, as some are in the habit of doing, but let us encourage one another—and all the more as you see the Day approaching" (Hebrews 10:24, 25). The Bible hints that the closer we get to the end of the world, the more difficult it will be for the Christian, and the more important it will be that we encourage one another. Jesus said:

> Then you will be handed over to be persecuted and put to death, and you will be hated by all nations because of me. At that time many will turn away from the faith and will betray and hate each other, and many false prophets will appear and deceive many people. Because of the increase of wickedness, the love of most will grow cold, but he who stands firm to the end will be saved (Matthew 24:9-13).

In the last days persecution will increase since Christians espouse values that the world hates. Apostasy will snowball as God's people get sucked into the world's system or become discouraged and quit. False teaching will be rampant as gullible people grope for something on which to build their lives. Temptations will multiply as wickedness increases; the Bible says that people will love the pleasures of this world more than they love God (2 Timothy 3:4).

There are indications that we are entering that era today. Opposition to Christianity is increasing, from government restrictions to ridicule in the media. Christians in many nations around the world are facing serious persecution. Temptations are intensifying as well: Television feeds a glamorized version of immorality and materialism right into our living rooms, and more and more communities are legalizing activities that until recently were detestable. And Christians are falling into apostasy: Mainline denominations that once stood for truth continue to deny the Bible is God's Word and bow the knee to expediency and compromise. Pews are empty and hearts are cold.

In this spiritual vacuum, people turn to cults and false religions. Eastern religions like Hinduism and Buddhism are popular even in America today, and Islam is, according to some experts, the fastest-growing religion in the world. Jesus asked, "When the Son of Man comes, will he find faith on the earth?" (Luke 18:8).

Thankfully, the Bible also promises that there will always be a remnant—not a majority, but a great multitude of believers nonetheless—who will maintain their commitment to Jesus Christ. As we enter potentially difficult times, it is vitally important that members of that remnant encourage and support one another.

> See to it, brothers, that none of you has a sinful, unbelieving heart that turns away from the living God. But encourage one another daily, as long as it is called Today, so that none

of you may be hardened by sin's deceitfulness. We have come to share in Christ if we hold firmly till the end the confidence we had at first (Hebrews 3:12-14).

I hope this chapter motivates you to encourage other believers. I'm not talking about boosting self-esteem, but encouraging others to be faithful to the Lord in this critical age.

Paul wrote about that kind of encouragement in his letter to the church in Thessalonica. They were facing intense opposition from the enemies of Christ. They were very much in the minority, and it wasn't easy to be a Christian. But Paul wrote an encouraging letter to them, saying:

> For you know that we dealt with each of you as a father deals with his own children, encouraging, comforting and urging you to live lives worthy of God, who calls you into his kingdom and glory.
>
> And we also thank God continually because, when you received the word of God, which you heard from us, you accepted it not as the word of men, but as it actually is, the word of God, which is at work in you who believe. For you, brothers, became imitators of God's churches in Judea, which are in Christ Jesus (1 Thessalonians 2:11-14).

Characteristics of an Effective Encourager

There are at least three characteristics that made Jesus an effective encourager.

Compassion

A man with leprosy came to Jesus and begged Him on his knees, "If you are willing, you can make me clean" (Mark 1:40). In Jesus' day leprosy was very contagious and deadly. A leper was therefore considered "unclean." By law he had to live outside the city and call out to anyone who approached, "Unclean! Unclean!"

That's why what Jesus did next is so noteworthy. "Filled with compassion, Jesus reached out his hand and touched the man," the Bible says (Mark 1:41). This man hadn't been touched by a human hand in days, probably years. In his book *Just Like Jesus*, Max Lucado imagined how the leper would tell the story:

> For five years no one touched me. No one. Not one person. Not my wife. Not my child. Not my friends. No one touched me. They saw me. They spoke to me. I sensed love in their voices. I saw concern in their eyes. But I didn't feel their touch. There was no touch. Not once. No one touched me.
>
> What is common to you, I coveted. Handshakes. Warm embraces. A tap on the shoulder to get my attention. A kiss on the lips to steal a heart. Such moments were taken from my world. No one touched me. No one bumped into me. What I would have given to be bumped into, to be caught in a crowd, for my shoulder to brush against another's. But for five years it has not happened. How could it? I was not allowed on the streets. Even the rabbis kept their distance from me. I was not permitted in my synagogue. Not even welcome in my own house.
>
> I was untouchable. I was a leper. And no one touched me. Until today.[24]

Jesus knew the man needed something even more than healing. He needed someone to say, "You're OK. Even with your disease, you still mean something. You're still valuable." He needed someone to heal his soul. Had Jesus only healed his leprosy, maybe the man would have grown bitter. *Why do people care about me again now that I'm whole?* he might have wondered. *What if I get another kind of disease? Must I go through that rejection again?* But Jesus reached out and touched him—while he was still a leper! And his life would never be the same again. How encouraging!

The first characteristic of an encourager is genuine compassion for those who need encouragement. When K. C. Jones was the coach of the Boston Celtics, he was known as an encourager, but he only encouraged his players when they needed it most. He rarely congratulated a player after a great play. When a player asked him about it, he said, "After hitting the winning shot, fifteen thousand people are cheering and players are high-fiving you. You don't need me then. When you need friends most is when no one else is cheering." Anyone can encourage the person who just won the game, just preached a great sermon, or just graduated. The person who needs encouragement is the one whom no one else is lifting up, who feels like he's been rejected.

When I was in college, I got a job working as a stock boy at the local A&P grocery store. I was grateful for a well-paying part-time job because I was paying my own way through school. One weekend I had worked all night long. Early in the morning, the district manager and store manager were working on a display in the front of the store. They saw me walking by with a two-wheel cart and asked me to take a stack of soda bottles from the old display to the back room. I wasn't very experienced with the two-wheel cart, and I didn't get the tray far enough under the stack. When I tried to lift the stack, it buckled. Bottles went flying and bursting everywhere. Some soda splashed up on the district manager's trousers as he jumped back. It took me a half hour to clean up the mess. I felt so incompetent and embarrassed.

About an hour later, I heard the manager's voice over the intercom: "Will Bob Russell please report to the office?" I knew I was about to be chewed out or maybe even fired. I walked into the office with my head hung low. The manager wasn't known as a great encourager, but he said, "Bob, we're a little shorthanded around here. If you know of any other young men from the Bible college who need work, please send them out here." That's all he said. It was his way of communicating that everything was OK. I don't know if he really needed more workers or just said that to boost me up, but the fact that he didn't fire me or even chew me out after such a bungle really encouraged me and restored my confidence.

Paul wrote, "And we urge you, brothers, . . . encourage the timid, help the weak, be patient with everyone" (1 Thessalonians 5:14). A great encourager is someone who has genuine compassion for those who are weak, sick, timid, or stumbling, and can sense that with a little boost, those who are downtrodden can turn things around to the glory of God. Paul himself was just such an encourager to the Thessalonians: "But we were gentle among you, like a mother caring for her little children," he reminded them (1 Thessalonians 2:7).

It's not just the weak who need compassion and encouragement. Sometimes it can be very lonely at the top, especially for those who must handle a lot of criticism. When Abraham Lincoln died, historians examined the contents of his wallet. In a corner pocket they found a yellowed newspaper clipping that had been opened and refolded so many times it was tearing at the edges. The clipping was from a newspaper editorial that suggested Lincoln would go down in history as a great president. Can't you just imagine Lincoln, after one of his many dark days when he felt beaten down by the world, taking out that clipping and reading it under the flicker of a lamp, being boosted up by one stranger who believed in him?

Someone mentioned "the lonely whine of the top dog." Don't assume that just because someone has reached the top by the world's standards he doesn't need any more encouragement. He needs to be reinforced that his efforts are worthwhile. Jesus encouraged Peter when he failed, but He also encouraged him when he succeeded. When Peter was bold enough to declare that Jesus was the Christ, Jesus said, "Blessed are you, Simon!" (Matthew 16:17). "Way to go, Peter! Good job! That's right!" Jesus encouraged him at his greatest triumph as well as in the moment of his heaviest defeat.

Action

It's one thing to feel compassion for someone. It's another thing to reach out and actually do something about it. A lot of people felt sorry for the leper, but only Jesus reached out and touched him. It was one thing for my boss to sense that I felt bad about spilling the display. He could have felt compassion for me and never shown it. When he called me into his office, his compassion turned to action, and that's what encouraged me.

Mike Breaux, who is a Teaching Pastor at the Willow Creek Community Church in South Barrington, Illinois, tells about a day several years ago, while he was the preacher in Harrodsburg, Kentucky, when he couldn't get Frank Wright off his mind. Frank was a schoolteacher and basketball coach at their local high school who had mentioned in passing to Mike, "Pray for me." Mike didn't know what the problem was, but he prayed for Frank and couldn't get him off his mind.

Then he decided to turn his compassion into action. He bought some balloons with cartoon characters on them and big letters that said, "Happy Birthday!" Mike had no idea when Frank's birthday was (he learned later it was three or four months earlier), but he walked into the school carrying those balloons, marched down the hall, interrupted Frank's class, and began to sing "Happy Birthday." The entire class enthusiastically joined in. At the end, Mike said, "Happy Birthday, Frank! We love you! Kids, let's all encourage Frank today!" And he walked out.

That night, Frank called Mike Breaux and said, "Mike, I don't know what got into you, but I needed that today. Thanks."

So many times we admire or respect someone, or we know someone who needs encouragement but we let the moment slip by. How do you know that God has not prompted you through His Holy Spirit to think of that person because he or she needs encouragement?

Selfless Motivation

Jesus said a strange thing after He healed the leper. The Gospel of Mark tells us Jesus sent him away with a strong warning: "See that you don't tell this to anyone. But go, show yourself to the priest and offer the sacrifices that Moses commanded for your cleansing, as a testimony to them" (1:44).

The leper didn't listen. Mark says he went and spoke freely about it to everyone he saw (1:45). Can you blame him? Even though the man didn't honor Jesus' request, the warning is significant because it reveals the heart of Christ. He wasn't performing this supernatural act just so He could draw more attention to himself. On the contrary, He did His best to deflect attention away from himself.

The Bible warns, "Whoever flatters his neighbor is spreading a net for his feet" (Proverbs 29:5). In the course of time, people can tell if you're encouraging them so they'll like you. They know if you're manipulating them so they'll perform better for you. Encouragement is meaningful if it's obvious you genuinely care for and appreciate the person.

I get my share of anonymous mail. I can tell you that most of the time it's not encouraging! Some time ago, a local clothier notified me that an anonymous donor had purchased a new suit for me. All I had to do was stop by and pick it up. I thought at first it was just a trick to get me in the store, but I discovered that someone had actually asked the salesman to call and invite me to come in for a new suit of my own selection!

The salesman said, "I can't tell you who it is, but you have a friend who says you have really ministered to him, and he wants to say thanks anonymously." I accepted the gracious offer. I reasoned that if Jesus accepted the expensive perfume poured on His feet, then surely I could accept a new suit! Whenever I put on that suit, I remember that gracious gift and I'm encouraged. It's been several years now since that event and I still don't know who gave me the suit, but the memory of that surprise anonymous gift is still an encouragement to me.

If you really want to make someone's day, send him or her a positive note or gift anonymously. As I mentioned in an earlier chapter, you keep your own ego out of it and ensure that the person who receives the encouragement knows it's sincere. Jesus challenged us:

Be careful not to do your "acts of righteousness" before men, to be seen by them. If you do, you will have no reward from your Father in heaven.

So when you give to the needy, do not announce it with trumpets, as the hypocrites do in the synagogues and on the streets, to be honored by men. I tell you the truth, they have received their reward in full. But when you give to the needy, do not let your left hand know what your right hand is doing, so that your giving may be in secret. Then your Father, who sees what is done in secret, will reward you (Matthew 6:1-4).

Some Practical Steps

I'm not the best encourager, but I've talked to people who are good at encouraging others. Here's what they suggest to combine your compassion with action and make your encouragement effective:

Be specific. When people say to me, "That was a good sermon," that's encouraging, but I wonder if they're just saying it out of habit. It's even better if they say, "I was really convicted by that part about controlling your tongue." Then I know they were really listening! Their specific encouragement means more.

Be occasional. After a while it's not that encouraging if someone gushes over you every time he sees you: "You look so nice today! You haven't aged a bit in thirty years! You're the greatest!" The Bible warns us to watch out for those who "by smooth talk and flattery . . . deceive the minds of naive people" (Romans 16:18). When Paul encouraged the Thessalonians he was determined not to use flattery (1 Thessalonians 2:5). If you gush over people all the time, it's not encouraging. Flattery may inflate the ego of a naive person, but it repulses the mature person. Instead of being a constant flatterer, be an occasional encourager.

Be balanced. The Bible says, "He who rebukes a man will in the end gain more favor than he who has a flattering tongue"

(Proverbs 28:23). Paul reminded Timothy and Titus that leading a church required them to "rebuke and encourage" (2 Timothy 4:2; Titus 2:15). Encouragement means more if it comes from someone who has cared enough about you to courageously tell you the truth on occasion, even when the truth wasn't pleasant.

Be genuine. A few years ago, I stepped off the platform after speaking at a convention and was greeted by the worship leader. As we talked, the woman who had sung a solo that night walked by us. He spoke to her, effusive with praise for her. I don't know a lot about music, but I thought she was below average. Yet he went on and on about how she had thrilled the audience. When she walked away, he mumbled to me, "It really wasn't very good, was it?" A few minutes later, when I turned to walk away, he said, "Hey, your sermon was outstanding tonight!" I wasn't very encouraged! Encouragement needs to be honest or eventually it will be empty. If you flippantly praise others, perceptive people will detect it as empty flattery and lose respect for you.

Write it down. It's nice to receive words of encouragement, but it means even more when people write it down. Our Preaching Associate Dave Stone once showed me a huge folder where he has kept notes and cards that people have sent him. He calls it his "Hang in There File." It's tougher to remember a verbal comment. So if you want to be an effective encourager, write it down.

Do it now. All of us have said, "I'm going to write a note someday and let them know how much that meant to me," but we don't get around to it and the opportunity passes by. The Bible says, "Be very careful, then, how you live—not as unwise but as wise, making the most of every opportunity, because the days are evil" (Ephesians 5:15, 16). If you want to be a great encourager, do it today!

9

Pray for One Another

I heard a preacher tell about a time when he was preaching and a little boy in the congregation was acting up, causing a distraction. The preacher prayed silently, "Lord, get that little boy for me." Just then the boy's father got up, put the boy under his arms, and began to carry him out. The boy called back to the congregation, "Pray for me!" The boy's prayer request wasn't answered, but the preacher's was!

In a much more serious situation, the night before Jesus went to the cross, He was agonizing over that which He knew He would soon endure. He took the disciples with Him and went to the Garden of Gethsemane to pray. Once they arrived, He said to them, "Sit here while I go over there and pray" (Matthew 26:36). The Bible says:

> He took Peter and the two sons of Zebedee along with him, and he began to be sorrowful and troubled. Then he said to them, "My soul is overwhelmed with sorrow to the point of death. Stay here and keep watch with me."
> Going a little farther, he fell with his face to the ground and prayed, "My Father, if it is possible, may this cup be taken from me. Yet not as I will, but as you will."

Then he returned to his disciples and found them sleeping. "Could you men not keep watch with me for one hour?" he asked Peter. "Watch and pray so that you will not fall into temptation. The spirit is willing, but the body is weak" (Matthew 26:37-41).

Jesus Asked for Prayer, But the Disciples Fell Asleep

In His final hour, the Son of God asked for prayer, but His best friends didn't deliver. They fell asleep. Matthew tells us why: "Their eyes were heavy" (26:43). You might be thinking, *How could they fall asleep at Jesus' most important hour? How could they let Him down?* I bet you can remember a time when your eyes were heavy and you couldn't seem to stay awake no matter how hard you tried.

I mentioned previously my all-night job in college working at the A&P store. I was also a weekend youth minister at Bridgetown Church of Christ in Cincinnati. When Sunday evening rolled around and it was time for the evening service, I was usually exhausted. One night Brother Irby was preaching and I just couldn't stay awake. I kept nodding off. Judy kept nudging me, trying to keep me from embarrassing myself. Afterward, one of the elders approached me and encouraged me to get more rest! I think it was his diplomatic way of saying, "If you want to stay on staff here, you'd be wise to stay awake during the senior minister's sermons!"

I suppose that wasn't as bad as the preacher who dreamed he was preaching, only to wake up and discover he *was* preaching!

I once conducted a devotional service for professional golfers after a long, hot day on the course. One golfer came in after a six-hour round during the heat of the day. The small room we were in wasn't well vented and soon got stuffy. As I talked, I could see this golfer's eyelids drooping. He worked hard to stay awake, but he was fighting a losing battle. Afterward he came up and said, "I really enjoyed your talk."

I wanted to say, "Yeah, I could tell you got a nice nap out of it!"

When I was growing up, my father worked two jobs and had a terrible time staying awake in church. He was one of the better Christians I've ever known. My memories of his struggles, combined with my own occasional difficulties staying awake, have made me more patient with people who fall asleep in church. Preachers can tell you about people drooling on their Bibles, snoring, and even bumping their heads on the pew in front of them. One guy was nudged awake by his wife and stood up to give the benediction!

Jesus was patient with His disciples when they fell asleep praying for Him. "The spirit is willing," He said, "but the body is weak" (Matthew 26:41). When He returned the second time and found them sleeping again, He didn't even try to wake them, but just went back to His anguishing prayers.

Intercessory Prayer

The Bible commands us to pray for one another (James 5:16). We call it "intercessory prayer." The reason we should intercede for one another is that prayer makes a difference. I recently completed writing a book entitled *When God Answers Prayer* in which I documented scores of real-life stories of answered prayer from people in our congregation and all over the world.[25] If Christians believe in the power of prayer and we love one another, how can we not pray for one another?

The Bible specifically mentions several categories of people for whom we should be praying.

Pray for Ministers, Missionaries, and Evangelists

Paul often asked his listeners to pray for him, that he might be able to continue preaching the Word of God boldly and clearly. "And pray for us, too," he asked the Colossians, "that God may open a door for our message, so that we may proclaim the mystery of Christ, for which I am in chains. Pray that I may proclaim it clearly, as I should" (4:3, 4). As he prepared to conclude his letter to the Thessalonians, he made a similar request of them: "Finally, brothers, pray for us that the message of the Lord may spread rapidly and be honored, just as it was with you. And pray that we may be delivered from wicked and evil men, for not everyone has faith" (2 Thessalonians 3:1, 2). He ended most of his letters in similar ways, constantly reminding his friends to pray for him and his ministry.

Whenever I get up to preach, a small group of people slip out of their pews and go into a side room to pray for me. For the entire thirty minutes, they are on their knees petitioning God to give me strength, wisdom, and courage, and to open the hearts of those who are hearing the Word of God being proclaimed. That's encouraging! I know that one of the biggest reasons God has blessed our congregation so much over the years is that from the time we were much smaller, members of the church have dedicated themselves to praying daily for the elders and ministers of our congregation.

Because we have a big church, it would be natural for other ministers to be envious of us. I know I battle envy when I think about churches like Willow Creek in Chicago and Saddleback in Southern California that are about the same size as we are and do some things better. However, preachers from other congregations often tell me they pray for me. I hope they're not praying for me as one of their enemies! I'm confident they are praying for me because they understand the pressure that comes from leading such a large group of people, and they want to see me succeed to the glory of God.

Our church recently raised $35 million in commitments for a new building and outreach project, exceeding our goal of $30 million. Mike Breaux, who was then the minister of the second-largest church in Kentucky, called to congratulate me. Just like his predecessor Wayne Smith, whom I mentioned earlier, Mike was, during his ministry at Southland, a constant encourager and supporter of Southeast's ministry. He left me a voice mail that said, "We want you to know we're thanking God for you and praising God for what He is doing through your church." Knowing that he was praying for us was a great encouragement to me.

Is your minister on your daily prayer list? How about his wife and children? Has your family adopted a missionary to pray for? What about a young person who might be considering going into the ministry? Like the apostle Paul who hungered for the prayers of his friends, ministers and their families long to know that people are petitioning God on their behalf.

Pray for Those Who Are Sick

Christians probably do a better job of praying for the sick than for any of the other categories of people mentioned in this chapter, yet I'm sure we could do better. Here are some clues to praying effectively for the sick.

Be specific. When you pray "for all the sick and those in prison," I'm sure God is pleased with your compassion for the suffering, but is anyone really helped by that prayer? Mention the individuals by name, and be specific in expressing to God what you are hoping will happen.

Recruit the elders for help. James wrote, "Is any one of you sick? He should call the elders of the church to pray over him and anoint him with oil in the name of the Lord" (5:14). The word translated "sick" in this passage suggests extreme illness. Though we are right to pray about any health problem, James says that when someone is battling serious illness, call in the spiritual leaders of the church for prayer.

When the elders join in prayer over the sick person, there is a special power that flows from God. In the next verse James promised, "And the prayer offered in faith will make the sick person well; the Lord will raise him up" (5:15).

James was not saying that the prayer of the elders is a magic formula that guarantees automatic healing of the body. Those who suggest otherwise are contradicting both Scripture and experience. Paul had the ability to heal the sick, yet he said, "I left Trophimus sick in Miletus," (2 Timothy 4:20) and he spoke of his own "thorn in the flesh" (2 Corinthians 12:7). Not every-one Paul prayed for was healed. We've anointed some people with oil and prayed for them, and they still died. We recently prayed for the healing of a young woman in her twenties who was battling cancer, but she still died. At her funeral, a visiting preacher mentioned how often she'd been prayed for and how disappointed we all were that she had not been healed. He added, "God chooses to make some people well; others He chooses to make perfect." Some of our prayers will not be fully answered until we get to Heaven and the Lord "raises us up."

But there are many others who have experienced dramatic answers for healing after the elders anointed them. In the book I wrote about answered prayer, I told the following story:

> Eleven-year-old Mary Whitlock had been experiencing seizures since she was five years old. Medicine and even brain surgery had not resolved the problem. In early sum-mer of 2002, she was having twenty to twenty-five seizures a day! Because of her condition she was not allowed to swim, attend parties, or do many other fun things with her friends that eleven-year-olds long to do.
>
> In August, just before school began, her Sunday school teacher Jim Hunt, who is also an elder in our church, sug-gested that the elders anoint her with oil and pray for her according to James 5:14. After the elders prayed, Mary's lit-tle sister added her own: "Please, God, don't let Mary have any more seizures." With the exception of one day when she battled strep throat, Mary Whitlock has not had a seizure since those prayers.[26]

We're not sure exactly what James meant when he com-manded the elders to anoint the sick person with oil. Was this anointing medicinal or ceremonial? It may have simply been symbolic of the presence of the Holy Spirit. When a very ill per-son in our congregation asks the elders to pray over him or her, a few of the elders will gather around, one will take a small amount of olive oil and touch the sick person's forehead with it, and then they will pray. In our situation, we are using the oil as a symbol of the presence of the Holy Spirit and a demonstration of our desire to be obedient to God. But the general feeling from Bible scholars about this passage is that the oil to which James referred was medicinal. Charles Swindoll wrote:

> The specific Greek term used in James 5:14 for anointing does not convey the thought of a religious ceremony in which oil is applied to the head. Here it means to "apply or to rub something into the skin." In biblical times, oil was used on one who was sick for its medicinal affects. We find this occurring in Luke 10:34 when the Samaritan poured oil and wine onto the wounds of the man victimized by robbers and left for dead.
>
> James does not write about ceremonial anointing; what he called for was the use of the best medicinal procedure of the day, simply rubbing or massaging oil into the body and then praying. Translating into today's terms, oil represents antibiotics, various other medications, surgery, therapy and so on.[27]

Instead of encouraging "faith healing" apart from the use of medicine, James taught the opposite: When you're sick, get the best medical treatment and apply it, then call for the most spiritual leaders of the church and have them pray.

Pray in faith. "And the prayer offered in faith will make the sick person well," James said (5:15). Does that mean if the person didn't get well, we didn't have enough faith? Not at all. As I mentioned before, Paul had the power to heal, but not even he had all his prayers for sick people answered affirmatively. Imagine the burden it would place on us if we knew all of our prayers would be answered just the way we asked them! No, we trust that God's ways are higher than ours, and He will do what is best. Offering a prayer in faith does not mean faith that we will get what we want—that's arrogance. The person who prays in faith believes that God will do what is best. In the same way that Jesus prayed, we should pray, "Lord, we would like to see this person made whole. Nevertheless, not our will, but yours be done. We know that we will not be made truly whole till eternity. We're offering this prayer in faith that you hear us and will do what is best."

Pray for the Persecuted

The Bible says, "Remember those in prison as if you were their fellow prisoners, and those who are mistreated as if you yourselves were suffering" (Hebrews 13:3). The writer of Hebrews didn't just want us to think about the persecuted with fond memories; he obviously intended that we remember them in our prayers. Years ago American Christians used to consider the persecuted church to be something in the past. But thanks to missionaries and groups like Voice of the Martyrs, we are now more aware of the persecuted church of today. We know that there were more Christian martyrs in the twentieth century than in the first nineteen centuries *combined*.[28] We are commanded to remember those who are suffering for their faith as if we ourselves were suffering. How would it feel? What must their families be enduring? What would they ask you to pray for if they could speak to you?

Maybe you could adopt a country where you know Christians are being persecuted—China, North Korea, Sudan, or one of many others—and pray that God will protect the Christians there, keep them strong in their faith, and grant them freedom.

As we write this book, the statues of Saddam Hussein are toppling in Iraq. On such historic occasions, we should remember to pray that missionaries are able to bring the gospel to those who have not yet heard and that the gospel finds fertile hearts. And we should thank God for the newfound freedom of secret Christians in Iraq. I saw footage of an Iraqi woman holding a sign on which she had scrawled, "Thank you, USA!" and making the sign of the cross. You could tell by the expression on her face that she was exuberant to be able to acknowledge Christ openly for the first time.

Pray for the Governing Authorities

Paul wrote:

> I urge, then, first of all, that requests, prayers, intercession
> and thanksgiving be made for everyone—for kings and all
> those in authority, that we may live peaceful and quiet
> lives in all godliness and holiness. This is good, and pleas-
> es God our Savior, who wants all men to be saved and to
> come to a knowledge of the truth (1 Timothy 2:1-4).

Praying for our government gained popularity after
September 11, 2001, when millions of people gathered in their
churches to pray for America. Max Lucado said, "Some evil
men sought to drive America to her knees that fateful day, but
they did not know the God to whom we pray when we are on
our knees." What Satan meant for evil, God has used for good
as Christians have faithfully and habitually prayed for America
since then.

I'm thankful that President George Bush asks for and seems
to appreciate the prayers of Christian people. It's important that
we pray not only for him, but for other leaders as well—members of congress, judges, members of city council, police officers,
and so on. Pray that those in authority will fear God, love righteousness, act justly, and live lives of integrity. The Proverbs
promise, "Righteousness exalts a nation, but sin is a disgrace to
any people" (14:34), and "When the righteous thrive, the people
rejoice; when the wicked rule, the people groan" (29:2).

It is easier to pray for your leaders when you helped vote
them into office. It's more difficult to pray for them when they
have a different ideology than you do, when you disagree with
many of the decisions that they make, or when their integrity is
in question. But remember the kind of culture in which Paul
was writing. They'd never heard of a "Christian" government.
They lived under a pagan Roman regime that was corrupt to
the core and at times persecuted them mercilessly. Yet Paul
commanded them to pray and even be thankful for those in
authority. In another passage he said the authorities that existed

got their power from God! (See Romans 13:1.) If Paul could have that kind of submissive spirit in praying for and thanking God for the Romans, how much more should we, even when our favorite party isn't in power? Remember, Jesus said to pray for your enemies, too! (Read the next section.) Regardless of party affiliation or lifestyle, those in authority need our prayers.

Pray for Your Enemies

Jesus said,

> "You have heard that it was said, 'Love your neighbor and hate your enemy.' But I tell you: Love your enemies and pray for those who persecute you, that you may be sons of your Father in heaven. He causes his sun to rise on the evil and the good, and sends rain on the righteous and the unrighteous. If you love those who love you, what reward will you get? Are not even the tax collectors doing that? And if you greet only your brothers, what are you doing more than others? Do not even pagans do that?" (Matthew 5:43-47).

Pray for your enemies? That's not very glamorous, and it certainly doesn't seem fair. Jesus not only commanded us to pray for our enemies, He modeled it for us. On the cross He prayed through parched lips for the ones who had inflicted agonizing pain on Him, saying, "Father, forgive them, for they do not know what they are doing" (Luke 23:34).

The Bible says, "Do not take revenge, my friends, but leave room for God's wrath, for it is written: 'It is mine to avenge; I will repay,' says the Lord" (Romans 12:19). Your judgment is skewed. It is not perfect. Only God is the perfect judge. David often prayed for justice for his enemies. For example, he wrote in Psalm 3:7: "Arise, O LORD! Deliver me, O my God! Strike all my enemies on the jaw; break the teeth of the wicked." In another song he wrote, "Arise, O LORD, in your anger; rise up against the rage of my enemies. Awake, my God; decree justice" (Psalm 7:6). David was honest in his prayers. He didn't want to be overcome by his enemies; he wanted God's justice to prevail. It wasn't a sin for David to communicate honestly with God about his feelings toward his enemies. He understood that only God could provide true justice. Jesus commanded us to take our prayers a step further. "Love your enemies," He said, "and pray for those who persecute you" (Matthew 5:44).

Paul commanded us to bless our enemies, saying, "Bless those who persecute you; bless and do not curse" (Romans 12:14). That's hard to do! When someone is assaulting you, cheating you in business, flirting with your wife, or treating your children unkindly, it's hard to pray, "Lord, please bless them"! However, that's what we are called to do. We can trust that God will make things right someday and His justice will ultimately prevail. Even more, God's will is for your enemy to surrender to Jesus and begin treating you kindly. Then everybody wins!

I got exasperated with the Hollywood celebrities who criticized President Bush's foreign policy during the war on Iraq. Many of them were caustic and disrespectful, even calling the president "a moron" and "stupid." I loved the e-mail I received pointing out that while the president and his cabinet each had a string of degrees from respected universities, almost all of the outspoken celebrities had only a high school education.

Then I read another e-mail that really convicted me. It asked, "How many of you who are disgusted with the Hollywood celebrities have prayed for them?" I certainly hadn't. I had criticized and ridiculed them, but had not even thought to pray that their eyes would be opened to the truth or their hearts would be softened for the gospel. They may have fame and wealth, but most of them don't have peace because they don't have Christ, and they need our prayers.

The Bible says, "If your enemy is hungry, feed him; if he is thirsty, give him something to drink. In doing this, you will heap burning coals on his head" (Romans 12:20). That sounds great at first—heaping burning coals on the heads of our enemies. The biblical expression, first found in Proverbs 25:22, probably refers to an ancient Egyptian custom whereby a repentant person would walk around with a basin of hot coals on his head to signify his regret. If so, the passage means that doing good to your enemy will cause him to feel bad about what he has done and repent of his ill behavior toward you.

Praying for your enemies is not only good for them, it's better for you because it helps you release your bitterness. "Bitterness is like acid," someone said. "It does more damage to the container in which it is stored than the object on which it is poured." Remember that when you pray for your enemies and seek to bless them, you release your bitterness, you give God a chance to work in their hearts to bring them to repentance, and everybody wins.

Pray for "One Another"

James commanded, "Therefore confess your sins to each other and pray for each other so that you may be healed. The prayer of a righteous man is powerful and effective" (5:16). Don't forget to pray for your fellow Christian friend who may not be a leader in the church or government, and may not be sick, but needs your prayers to remain faithful. I love the prayer that Paul offered for his good friends in the church at Philippi. He mentioned that he thanked God for them every time he thought of them, and that he always prayed with joy for them. Then he wrote:

> And this is my prayer: that your love may abound more and more in knowledge and depth of insight, so that you may be able to discern what is best and may be pure and blameless until the day of Christ, filled with the fruit of righteousness that comes through Jesus Christ—to the glory and praise of God (Philippians 1:9-11).

Are you praying for your mate—that her love for Christ will continue to abound—that she will grow in knowledge and depth of insight and be pure and blameless till the coming of Christ? Are you remembering to pray for your best friend— that he will be able to discern what is best when he makes decisions about his career, his marriage, and his family life? Are you praying for your children—that they may continue to be pure and blameless and be molded into the people God wants them to be? Are you interceding for your neighbor, asking God to fill him with the fruit of righteousness?

Jesus prayed for each of us, ". . . that all of them may be one, Father, just as you are in me and I am in you. May they also be in us so that the world may believe that you have sent me" (John 17:21). Jesus longs for us to be united. One of the best ways to accomplish the unity He longs for is to unite in prayer.

A couple of years ago, our church began hosting a quarterly Pastor's Prayer Luncheon. We invited preachers, staff members and church leaders from every church of every background in our community to come and pray together. We said the qualification was that we were going to pray "in Jesus' name." If you could come and pray in Jesus' name, then you were welcome. At each luncheon, we have over one hundred church leaders get together. We worship differently, we think differently, we look different, and we pray differently, but we are united in Jesus Christ. It has been a wonderful experience and a powerful testimony to the community for us to gather regularly to pray for one another and for our community.

One day I closed the prayer time by saying, "I want us all to get in a huge circle." I put a single chair in the center of the circle and said, "Now we're going to sing some choruses. As we sing, if you have a personal need, I'd like for you to sit down in this chair. We'll stop singing and we'll pray together for you."

I wondered if anyone would sit in the chair, but one after another, a minister would sit down as we sang. When we stopped singing, the minister would express a prayer need and we would designate someone to pray. After the prayer, we would start singing again.

It was a wonderful time of prayer. You could feel a sense of brotherly love, unity, and the power of the Holy Spirit at work. There we all were—black and white, charismatic and liturgical, young and old, men and women—praying together in the name of Jesus for one another. I wondered, though, how I should end the prayer time. I finally decided to sit down in the chair myself to conclude our time together. When I could tell an adequate amount of time had passed, I sat down. When the song ended, I said, "I'd like for you to pray that I will have the wisdom to lead this group and the courage to go wherever the Lord leads. Who will pray for me?" A charismatic preacher raised his hand.

About a third of the preachers who come to the luncheon are charismatic, and another third are from primarily African-American congregations. Both of those groups pray differently than I am used to praying—they affirm each other in prayer. I was taught to pray silently while others are praying aloud, but they pray on top of each other. I'm not used to it, but I know God has the ability to hear each of our prayers whether we're talking over one another or all praying silently. To those who are used to that kind of praying, it isn't awkward, disorganized, or disrespectful. So the charismatic preacher laid his hands on me and began praying for me as the others affirmed his prayer. "Lord," he prayed, "this man has asked for wisdom. Don't give it to him! He wouldn't know what to do with it! You *be* his wisdom! Fill his mind with Your thoughts and desires."

The others said, "Amen! Yes, Lord!"

He continued, "This man has asked for courage. Don't give it to him! You *be* his courage, Lord. You be his strength." The other preachers again affirmed his prayer.

I can't say that anything dramatic happened at the end of that prayer service. I can tell you that the Spirit of God continues to work in our community, not just in our congregation but also in hundreds of others to bring people to Jesus Christ. A preacher from my background later said to me, "Russell, I can't think of a more unlikely person to be in the center of that group, but it was wonderful how the Lord used prayer to bring us all together." There is a great spirit of unity among Bible-believing Christians in Louisville, Kentucky, and I think we have to attribute much of that unity to the fact that we have prayed for one another.

10

Be Kind to One Another

Christian humorist Dennis Swanberg says one of his favorite stories happened to him on Easter Sunday in Saginaw, Texas, several years ago. The church was packed for Easter services. The high school basketball coach was in the middle of giving his testimony when water started dripping through the ceiling onto the choir. The air conditioning units were in the attic and the condensation pans were overflowing, causing water to drip down through the ceiling. Two men got up and went out the side door. Swanberg says, "They could have just turned off the air conditioning units, but no. They got to go up there and fix that thing, try to be heroes!" Soon you could hear them walking across the ceiling joists in the attic. Swanberg said, "You've heard of it happening—it happened. Whoosh!" One of them came through the ceiling. He grabbed the joists and held on for dear life. The crowd gasped. The man's mother, sitting in the "afghan division," recognized her son's chubby legs and hollered out his name.

Swanberg looked at the coach, whose microphone was still on. "Only preachers can pray this fast," Swanberg recalls. "I prayed, 'Lord, don't let him say something he'd say on the basketball court!' Not that he would, but he could—we're all human."

The coach looked at Swanberg and said, "Brother Dennis, are we having a healing service—someone coming through the roof?" The crowd roared with laughter.

The man's friend helped him back up onto the joists and everything turned out fine. The service went on, although Swanberg says nobody listened much to the sermon. They were all just staring at that hole in the roof.

At the end of the service, Swanberg stood at the back of the church to shake hands "and be pastoral." The first guy to shake his hand was a rancher who only came at Easter. He said, "Brother Dennis, I told my wife there's no need for me to go to church. Told her if I did, the roof would cave in. Sure 'nough it did!"

Mark chapter two records that dramatic healing service the basketball coach was talking about where four men brought their friend who was paralyzed to Jesus and found the only way to get him to the Master was through the roof. It's a great story that should teach us some things about being kind to one another.

Paralyzed by an Infirmity

A few days later, when Jesus again entered Capernaum, the people heard that he had come home. So many gathered that there was no room left, not even outside the door, and he preached the word to them. Some men came, bringing to him a paralytic, carried by four of them (Mark 2:1-3).

The Bible doesn't elaborate on the cause of this man's condition. I wish we knew more about him. Had he been born paralyzed? Did he have polio or severe arthritis? Was he injured in an accident? Had he fallen off a roof? Had he experienced a stroke that left him unable to walk? Maybe he'd been in a fight in a bar and was seriously wounded or was the victim of a mugging in the marketplace. We don't know why he was paralyzed, but we know he couldn't walk.

Several years ago at a week of Christian service camp, we had a "Handicap Awareness Day." We assigned every camper a disability for a four-hour period. One was in a wheelchair. Another was blindfolded and had to be led around by friends. Another had earplugs. One had tape over his mouth. (I personally selected the camper for that role!) Some walked on crutches. Others had an arm tied to their side so they could relate to an amputee. The campers had to play ball, go through the dinner line, and listen to lessons while "suffering" from their disabilities. Our hope was that they would gain appreciation for the challenges faced by those with disabilities and be motivated to express kindness to people who have disabilities.

Have you ever pondered what it would be like to be permanently disabled? What's it like to be blind—to miss the facial expressions of those you love, the bursting of spring, sporting events, the colors of the rainbow? What's it like to be deaf—to see people moving their lips and laughing and wonder what they're saying? What's it like to have a mental disability and not be able to read?

Jennifer Heck is a delightful young lady in our church who was born with cerebral palsy. Though her muscles don't work right, her mind is brilliant. She once gave her testimony to our teenagers and told them about her disability. Complications at birth, she explained, "caused brain damage affecting my motor center, resulting in my speech impediment and spasticity." She confessed:

> I knew I was different from the other kids, but I also knew deep down that I was very much the same. We all know that growing up is painful. I faced kids mocking and staring because of the way I walk and talk. I learned to grin and bear it, but I would lock myself in my bedroom and cry. I cried a lot growing up, because I wanted people to look beyond my disability and know me as a person.

Thankfully Jesus Christ has made a difference in Jennifer's life, and she has learned to praise Him in spite of and even through her disability. I can't imagine how frustrating it must be for her at times to have the words flowing out of her mind and not be able to get them out of her mouth, or to have to take so long to peck them out on a keyboard.

Assisted by Friends

Though he couldn't walk, the man who was paralyzed in Mark 2 was blessed to have friends who cared enough about him to carry him. "Some men came," Mark writes, "bringing to him a paralytic, carried by four of them" (v. 3).

At least four men expressed kindness to this man who was paralyzed. Warren Wiersbe, in his commentary, points out several admirable characteristics of these men.[29]

They were deeply concerned about their friend and wanted to see him helped. It's exhausting to lug a heavy man on a stretcher for any distance, but these friends were kind enough to exert the effort for the sake of their companion in need.

They had faith to believe that Jesus could meet his need. They had heard reports of Jesus healing others who couldn't walk. They believed that Jesus was the primary hope for their bedfast friend. The ultimate kindness is to bring someone to Jesus.

They didn't permit the crowd around Jesus to discourage them. When they arrived, there were so many people crowded into the house and even on the outside that there was no way to get through to Jesus.

Sometimes even today people who are disabled can't get to Jesus because the crowd around Him blocks the way. Jim Pierson, founder of the Christian Church Foundation for the Handicapped, says that 90 percent of people who are disabled don't go to church anywhere. One reason is that people block the way. "I came to church, but I got the coldest stares in the lobby." "I went to a class, but people avoided me and it was awkward." "I couldn't get into the building because they only had steps and no wheelchair ramp." "I couldn't go to the rest-room because of the narrow doors." The four friends of this man who was paralyzed refused to get discouraged when the crowd blocked the way.

They worked together and dared to do something different. Mark describes what happened next: "Since they could not get him to Jesus because of the crowd, they made an opening in the roof above Jesus and, after digging through it, lowered the mat the paralyzed man was lying on" (2:4).

Houses in that day often had flat roofs that were accessible by an outside stairway. The men lugged their friend up the steps, trying to keep him parallel and comfortable, and then began removing the twigs and grass that comprised the roof. That was risky! They were interrupting Jesus' sermon down below. Some dirt and limbs were bound to fall through onto the crowd below and irritate those who got dirt in their hair. They could be rebuked for tearing up the roof and forced to make repairs, but they were determined to find healing for their friend.

Sometimes acts of kindness are risky. Your actions could be misunderstood or your motives could be questioned. The receiver of your act of generosity may not appreciate it. He may even be offended by it. But the Bible says, "Love is kind" (1 Corinthians 13:4). When you love someone, you're willing to take some risks to express kindness to him or her.

One of the most pressing needs of a person with disabilities is friendship. He needs someone who will be kind enough to make eye contact and not look away. She needs someone who will kindly stop and strike up a conversation. One disabled man told a counselor at our church that he enjoyed going to the dentist because that was the one place he was touched. People with disabilities need friends who will listen patiently even though it may take longer to get the words out; they need people who will touch them without being repulsed.

Transformed by Jesus

Jesus and those around Him felt dirt falling from the ceiling above. They looked up and realized there was quite a commotion on the roof. The crowd did their best to back out of the way lest more than dirt fall on their heads! In a matter of moments, here came a man through the roof!

Dennis Swanberg says, "I used to picture these four men slowly lowering the man down by four ropes—each one holding a corner—and perfectly placing him down in front of Jesus." Then he says, "Come on, people! Those were deacons! They probably wrapped him up like Gulliver's Travels and he came swirling down in front of Jesus. Jesus had to catch him and help lower him down."

I imagine Swanberg is right. They probably removed as little of the roof as possible, quickly wrapped him up as best they could and began to lower him down feet first with a rope wrapped around the mat and his body. I imagine Jesus with a big grin on His face helping to lower the man down.

When Jesus saw their faith, He said to the man who was paralyzed, "Son, your sins are forgiven" (Mark 2:5). That sounds like a strange thing for Jesus to say to a man who is hoping to be healed of his paralysis. If you went to a doctor with numbness on your left side and after examining you he said, "Your sins are forgiven!" you'd probably be perturbed. Why did Jesus say this first?

He said this perhaps because the man's paralysis was a direct result of sin in his life. Maybe in a drunken stupor he'd fallen off a horse and injured his spine. Maybe he'd been immoral and contacted a social disease that left him physically impaired. Maybe he'd become so depressed he had tried to end his life by jumping off a cliff and wound up a quadriplegic. The man may have not only been physically paralyzed, but paralyzed by guilt and shame as well because of his past. Jesus knew that kindness meant expressing to the man that he could be forgiven and accepted regardless of his past.

Jesus may have forgiven his sins to illustrate what is most important. We don't read about the man again in the Gospels, but we know what happened to him: eventually, he died. When he stood before God, the most important thing in his life was not that Jesus had healed him, but that Jesus had saved him. By forgiving his sins, Jesus was granting him eternal life with God. That was the kindest thing Jesus could do for him.

Jesus may have made this statement to confirm His own deity. Mark goes on to explain, "Now some teachers of the law were sitting there, thinking to themselves, 'Why does this fellow talk like that? He's blaspheming! Who can forgive sins but God alone?'" (2:6).

Jesus knew what they were thinking, so He asked them, "Why are you thinking these things? Which is easier: to say to the paralytic, 'Your sins are forgiven,' or to say, 'Get up, take your mat and walk'?" (Mark 2:8, 9). Anyone can say, "Your sins are forgiven," but that doesn't prove he has the authority to forgive sins. But if a man said to a person who is paralyzed, "Your sins are forgiven," and then said, "Rise up and walk," then he would prove his supernatural power and authority. So Jesus continued, "But that you may know that the Son of Man has authority on earth to forgive sins . . . ." He said to the man who was paralyzed, "I tell you, get up, take your mat and go home" (Mark 2:10, 11).

The Bible says, "He got up, took his mat and walked out in full view of them all. This amazed everyone and they praised God, saying, 'We have never seen anything like this!'" (Mark 2:12). They had to admit—Jesus is unique. If He can do that, He has the power to forgive sins.

The Application for Us

The Bible says, "Be kind and compassionate to one another, forgiving each other, just as in Christ God forgave you" (Ephesians 4:32), and elsewhere, "For this very reason, make every effort to add . . to godliness, brotherly kindness; and to brotherly kindness, love" (2 Peter 1:5-7).

I can think of at least three groups of people toward whom we should be kind as we seek to imitate Jesus Christ.

Be Kind to Those with Disabilities

One of the ways Christians should express kindness is to be like the friends in this story and extend it to those who are disabled. Professional football coach and commentator Dan Reeves said, "You can tell the character of a man by the way he treats those who can do nothing for him." The Bible says, "He who oppresses the poor shows contempt for their Maker, but whoever is kind to the needy honors God" (Proverbs 14:31).

I mentioned earlier my friend Jennifer Heck who has cerebral palsy. Jennifer is an excellent writer. She sent me an article she wrote for a Christian magazine in which she suggested several ways we can treat kindly those with disabilities:

> See the "person," not the disability. . . . Focus on the similarities you share—namely that one God created both of you as precious people in His sight and you both need His life-changing truth and love.
>
> Initiate. Many people with disabilities have not had the opportunity to develop social skills or outgoing personalities. Therefore, I encourage you to seek them out and let them know that you want to get to know them.
>
> Fine-tune your listening skills. It may take more effort and patience in communication. Try blocking out the surroundings so the person feels that you are sincerely focusing on him or her.
>
> Be honest. If you don't understand what the person says or means, tell him or her. Don't pretend to understand.
>
> Make eye contact. Eye contact is vital in relationships. Looking people in their eyes communicates that you are not afraid of them and are interested in what they are saying.
>
> Offer a ride. Transportation is a major reason people with disabilities are not coming to church.[30]

Be Kind to Those Who Are Close to You

Why is it that the hardest place to be kind to others is at home? The people we love the most are usually the ones we treat most unkindly.

A preacher friend of mine related to me that he and his wife had a serious argument. He couldn't take it anymore, so he stormed out of the house and went for a drive. While he was riding around, he noticed that the car in front of him had a nearly flat tire. He followed the car until it stopped at a shopping center. He pulled beside the car, and when the woman driving it got out, he said to her, "Ma'am, I just wanted you to know that your left rear tire is nearly flat."

She looked and said, "Thank you very much. That was really kind of you to let me know."

He said at first he felt good about the kindness he had shown. Then he thought, *Why can I go out of my way to be kind to a stranger and yet I can be such a thoughtless bozo to my wife?* The people we're the closest to are the ones who need common everyday courtesies, yet they are the least likely to receive our acts of kindness.

Be Kind to Strangers in the Name of Christ

Steve Sjogren wrote a thought-provoking Christian book a few years ago entitled *Conspiracy of Kindness*.[31] He trained his church to create opportunities for evangelism through simple deeds of compassion and kindness. For example, members of his church bought several hundred cartons of soft drinks and stood on the corner of a busy intersection handing out free cold drinks. They said to the recipients, "This is just a tangible way for us to say Jesus cares about you." People in his church often volunteer to wash cars free of charge in the name of Christ—no donations allowed. They will go into restaurants and even bars and ask the owner if they can clean the restrooms for him. The dumbfounded owner will often respond, "Whatever turns you on." They rent space at a shopping center at Christmastime and wrap presents for free, saying, "This gift is wrapped for you by

Christians who care." Sjogren says that kindness is so rare that people are impressed when they see a tangible demonstration of God's love. He says we've made evangelism much too difficult. We've got all kinds of organized programs, but, "We need more high touch," he says, "and not so much high tech."

I think he's right. I heard a preacher wisely say, "It would be amazing how many people we could influence for Christ if we would just treat them nicely." Jesus said, "And if anyone gives even a cup of cold water to one of these little ones because he is my disciple, I tell you the truth, he will certainly not lose his reward" (Matthew 10:42).

Kindness can't just be a temporary act we put on to impress other people. It needs to be a garment we wear constantly—a continuous virtue that is a part of the fabric of our lives. The Bible says, "Therefore, as God's chosen people, holy and dearly loved, clothe yourselves with compassion, kindness, humility, gentleness and patience" (Colossians 3:12).

Endnotes

[1] Roy Angell was a great old Baptist preacher from Miami, Florida, almost a century ago. He was a brilliant biblical expositor. Back before World War II, he preached on this Samaritan story.

[2] William Barclay, *The Daily Study Bible Series: The Gospel of John*, Revised Edition, Volume 1 (Philadelphia: Westminster Press, 1975), p. 162.

[3] Robert C. Shannon, *Christ Above All* (1989). Information retrieved in June 2003 from <u>dabar.org/Homiletics/Above/Ch15.htm</u> on the World Wide Web.

[4] *Our Daily Bread*, December 28, 1998.

[5] "Good Deeds Do You Good," *Reader's Digest*, April 2003, p. 182.

[6] Dr. Dan Garcia, *Louisville Medicine* (Bulletin for the Jefferson County Medical Society), Volume XXXVIII, No. 7, December 1990, pp. 27, 28.

[7] C. S. Lewis, *A Grief Observed*, copyright © C.S. Lewis Pte. Ltd. 1961. Extract reprinted by permission.

[8] Elisabeth Kubler-Ross, *On Death and Dying* (New York: Macmillan, 1969).

[9] Haddon Robinson, "Grief" (pamphlet published by the Christian Medical Society for Zondervan Corporation, 1974), pp. 11-16.

[10] Ibid, p. 11.

[11] Ibid, p. 13.

[12] Barbara Roberts, *Death Without Denial, Grief Without Apology* (Troutdale, OR: New Sage Press, 2002).

[13] C. S. Lewis, *A Grief Observed*, copyright © C.S. Lewis Pte. Ltd. 1961. Extract reprinted by permission.

[14] Dr. Cyril J. Barber, *Through the Valley of Tears*, p. 26. Information retrieved in June 2003 from <u>plymouthchurchwhittier.com/ cyril/entirebook.pdf</u> on the World Wide Web.

[15]Haddon Robinson, "Grief," p. 16.

[16]Charles Dickens, *Great Expectations*, p. 178. Information retrieved in June 2003 from literaturepage.com/read/greatexpectations-178.html on the World Wide Web.

[17]Robert Louis Stevenson, *Edinburgh Picturesque Notes*. Information retrieved in June 2003 from authorsdirectory.com/c/edinn10.htm on the World Wide Web.

[18]Edwin Markham, "Outwitted," *The Best Loved Poems of the American People* (1936), p. 67. Information retrieved in June 2003 from english.uiuc.edu/maps/poets/m_r/markham/poems.htm on the World Wide Web.

[19]James Collins, *Good to Great* (New York: Harper Business, 2001), pp. 28, 29.

[20]Ibid, pp. 27, 28.

[21]Skeptics used to criticize the Bible's accounts of the healing of Bartimaeus because there seems to be a contradiction. Matthew and Mark record that Jesus is leaving Jericho while Luke says that He is approaching Jericho. There are several possible explanations for the differences, but it can most likely be speculated in light of recent archaeological discoveries that Jesus was traveling between the "old Jericho" and the "new Jericho." We now know there were two Jerichos, just as there is an old English, Indiana, and a new English, Indiana. (The town in Indiana was moved because of frequent flooding.) The apparent contradiction only adds to the credibility of Scripture, proving that the authors did not corroborate.

[22]Ken Gire, *Incredible Moments with the Savior* (Grand Rapids, MI: Zondervan, 1990), p. 105.

[23]Ibid, p. 106.

[24]Max Lucado, *Just Like Jesus* (Nashville, TN: Word Publishing, 1998), pp. 29, 30.

[25]Bob Russell, *When God Answers Prayer* (West Monroe, LA: Howard Publishing, 2003).

[26]Ibid, p. 94.

[27]Chuck Swindoll, *Bible Study Guide: James* (Fullerton, CA: Charles R. Swindoll, 1983), p. 84.

[28]Nina Shea, *In the Lions' Den: Persecuted Christians and What the Western Church Can Do About It* (Nashville: Broadman & Holman), back cover.

[29]Warren Wiersbe, *The Bible Expository Commentary*, Volume 1 (Colorado Springs, CO: Chariot Victor Publishing, 1989), p. 115.

[30]Jennifer Heck, "New Perspective: Everyone Benefits by Including People with Disabilities," *Key to Christian Education*, Winter 1995, pp. 8, 9.

[31]Steve Sjogren, *Conspiracy of Kindness: A Refreshing New Approach to Sharing the Love of Jesus Christ with Others* (Ann Arbor, MI: Vine Books, 1993).